PRAISE FOR *TAKE CONTROL*

"I've seen Rickson evolve from driven advisor to Whole Person. *Take Control* distills that transformation into a practical, honest roadmap for advisors seeking relief from hidden struggles, misaligned goals, and burnout. This book shows the path to clarity, purpose, and true success."

— Brian D. Heckert, 2016 MDRT President
MDRT Member for 37 years | Top of the Table: 18 years
Managing Director | Senior Advisor, FSM Wealth, Inc.

"I've been lucky enough to know Rickson long before he became the ultra-marathon version of himself. Back then, he was one hundred and thirty-eight kilos. Today, he signs up for races that make the rest of us question our life choices. I'll stick to dancing. It is safer.

This transformation taught me something: when Rickson commits to something, physics itself seems negotiable.

But here's what really impressed me in forty years of this business: Rickson knows his WHY. Not the corporate mission statement version that sounds good in meetings. The real one. The kind that gets you out of bed when bed seems like the better option.

He takes that same relentless approach with his clients' financial futures. He'll work himself into the ground for the right people. Notice I said, 'right people.' Because Rickson does something most advisors won't: he says no. If you're not serious about your financial independence, he'll show you the door. Politely. But firmly.

I've spent four decades in insurance and wealth management, and I'm supposed to be the mentor here. The truth? I learn from Rickson constantly. He absorbs new ideas like a sponge, implements them like a machine, and shares everything he learns with anyone who'll listen.

This book is pure Rickson. No fluff. No magic formulas. Just hard-won lessons from someone who walked the walk, literally and financially. He transformed his body, built a thriving practice, and figured out what actually matters in life.

He's going to challenge you. Good. You'll be better for it."

— Ashok Sardana
MDRT Member for 33 years | Top of the Table: 28 years
Managing Director, Continental Insurance Brokers & Financial Services

"I first heard Rickson speak at TOT 2023.

At that instant, I was blown away: How does someone serve only four clients a year, clear multiple TOTs, and still live so fully?

Rickson's philosophy of life and work completely redefined how I work.

Since then, I've been inspired to clear my TOT while working on other life projects—my health, quality family time, giving back to the industry, and fostering meaningful relationships.

What has always stood out about Rickson is his generosity. When I was in Dubai for MDRT Global, he hosted my entire team and shared insights with a sincerity that's rare in our industry.

This is the same sincerity that runs through every chapter of this book.

Take Control is not just another 'mindset book.' It's a full framework. Rickson breaks down what real mastery looks like: crystal-clear goals, extreme ownership, knowing your numbers with brutal honesty, and building a practice around right-fit clients instead of hustle culture.

His C.O.N.T.R.O.L. model is simple yet profound, and every chapter comes with practical steps, real stories, and hard-earned lessons that only a true practitioner can teach.

What I appreciate most is how actionable the book is. The systems, checklists, mindset shifts, and even the TLDR sections make it easy for any adviser, regardless of whether you're a rookie or experienced advisor, to implement immediately.

This is the kind of guide I wish had existed when I started.

Take Control is a must-read for anyone who wants exponential growth without losing themselves in the process."

— Jaslyn Ng
MDRT Member for 8 years | Top of the Table: 3 years
Financial Services Director, Prudential Assurance Company Singapore

"Rickson is one of the rare individuals who leads with both mastery and heart. His guidance has influenced how I run my own financial advisory practice, and his generosity as a friend and mentor never fails to inspire. *Take Control* distills the very mindset and discipline that define him—honest, focused, and transformational. If you want clarity and exponential growth in both business and life, read this book."

— Cheng Huann Yeoh
MDRT Member for 13 years | Court of the Table: 5 years
Senior Director, Great Eastern Financial Advisers Private Limited

"*Take Control* is a masterclass in intentional growth. Most of the books I read have a little bit of steak and a lot of sizzle. This book is all signal and no noise. Rickson does a great job outlining what needs to be done to take control of your career and life—and win big on both fronts."

— Matthew Abrams
Expert EOS Implementor™, EOS Worldwide®

TAKE CONTROL

THE FINANCIAL ADVISOR'S GUIDE TO EXPONENTIAL INCOME GROWTH

TAKE CONTROL

THE FINANCIAL ADVISOR'S GUIDE TO EXPONENTIAL INCOME GROWTH

Rickson Dsouza

CoVerse
COLLECTIVE

Published by Igniting Souls
PO Box 43, Powell, OH 43065
IgnitingSouls.com

Paperback ISBN: 978-1-63680-586-3
Hardback ISBN: 978-1-63680-587-0
eBook ISBN: 978-1-63680-588-7

Available in paperback, hardcover, e-book, and audiobook.

To Sangeeta, Leiah, and Luca,
In a world of moving pieces, you are my constant.

CONTENTS

FOREWORD BY DAN SULLIVAN

Rickson Dsouza moved fast, his sights set on possibilities that most only dream about but never pursue. Each step pushed him past hesitation; every choice seemed charged with purpose and set in motion by something invisible yet powerful.

He focused on what mattered, challenge after challenge, obsessed by numbers, energized by the right clients, and relentless in extracting meaning from setbacks.

Observing Rickson in action, you can't help but wonder: what is driving this rhythm, and how does he always find momentum when others stall?

The answer starts long before that decisive sprint, back in the quiet moment when Rickson chose to claim ownership of his future while most waited, hoping for conditions to change. He realized progress is crafted by creators, not spectators.

Rickson turned big ideas into tangible steps, learned through risks—racing across deserts, shaping businesses, and building a life that worked by his design.

He refused to be at the mercy of fate, flipped every failure into fuel, and discovered in the C.O.N.T.R.O.L. framework the map for lasting growth. Clear goals, fearless ownership, data-driven numbers, well-timed tactics, right-fit clients, passionate obsession, and a life lived with intention. Rickson's breakthroughs came from refusing excuses, from turning "Why not me?" into "What's next for me?"

Now, at the end of this journey, the story reinforces why Rickson's path compels attention and wins respect. The rhythm that began with curiosity, then accelerated with action, now reveals an answer you can claim for yourself: ownership, mastery, and momentum aren't reserved for the lucky or risk-free. They live in every deliberate move you make, in refusing to wait, and in building a blueprint where your business and life amplify each other.

Rickson shows the way.

The question is no longer "Why him?" but instead, "Why not you?" You know the answer. The next step is yours.

— Dan Sullivan, Co-Founder of Strategic Coach®

PREFACE: WHY I WROTE THIS BOOK

How do you condense 25 years of experience and lessons learned into a few chapters? I didn't know, but I had to try. And so, I began writing this book as I do most things in my life with Stephen R. Covey's astute advice ringing in my head: "Begin with the end in mind."

I have been sharing my content in the digital world through social media and delivering my message on stages all over the world for a few years now. Everything I share in those spaces is valid. It holds. On many occasions, I've even been told that it has helped make a significant mark, drive change, or allowed a financial advisor or a team to shift gears from incremental growth to exponential growth and achievement.

While that delights me and is something I'll keep doing for years to come, I felt the need to condense my biggest lessons into one place. And that was the 'end' I had in mind for this project.

I wanted to create a quick read that you could pick up and go through in one afternoon and, on the back of it, take real, tangible action to transform your life and career. I wanted to create, in other words, a quick and easy guide for you to experience exponential growth in your life and career.

With that intention in mind, I've taken the liberty to go completely against the grain. This is a recurring theme that you will find in this book, too. I almost always go against the grain. I like to question the status quo, asking 'Why' in rooms where established ideas and ways of doing things have taken hold, and wondering how things could be done better, faster, and more optimally. As a result, I've managed to create some results that would have knocked 21-year-old-me's socks right off.

But I digress. What I mean here by going against the grain is that most books and most authors focus on 'one thing.' The publishers and the booksellers tell you that it will be much easier to sell if the focus is on ONE message, ONE focus area, and ONE main piece of advice.

In my experience, however, transformation isn't one-dimensional. Transformation is the result of many micro-shifts in your mindset and your actions. Transformation is the culmination of every moment where you make the harder choice, stick with the plan, or put in one more 'rep,' literally and hypothetically.

These tiny shifts and decisions culminate in the ultimate naked-eye shift that everybody sees:

You've shed 50 pounds and look half your size!

You've gone from beginner to top performer on your sales team in a few months!

You're energised, fun, light, and great to be around instead of the stressed-out workaholic you were a couple of years ago!

Whatever other 'after' state that you're after, I'm here to tell you from firsthand experience: All of that is possible for you. Even your wildest dreams are within your reach. But it's going to take some work. And more importantly, it's going to take a methodology.

Over the next few chapters, I'll outline my methodology for bringing about transformation and achieving massive goals in my career and life. I'm certain this is not the only route to setting and smashing exponential goals, but it has proven successful for me time and time again.

There is one other reason I decided to pen this methodology down: I'm an avid reader and content consumer. I love a good podcast episode, a good documentary, and a good article. But I also know just how long it's taken me to tailor my content diet to one that serves me. As opposed to the problems our forefathers faced—slow, limited, or no access to information outside of their immediate community and surroundings—we have the exact opposite: a more dire problem. We have way too much access to way too much information – most of it unverifiable.

That's an extremely dangerous landscape. Don't get me wrong – I love the landscape, and I'm a contributor to that landscape, too. But it's dangerous because it is designed to keep pulling you into the next rabbit hole, the next click, the next occasion when you whip out your credit card to pay for something you've been made to think you need.

It's not unlikely that you end up buying a program called 'How to Optimise Your Time and Get More Done in an Hour' and 'How to Procrastinate for Productivity'—both products filled with promises that they will carry you to the promised land. No wonder so many people are stuck 'learning' how to achieve rather than getting out there and achieving.

The good news is that I've probably consumed both programs and all the others that might appeal to you as you grow professionally and personally. Following that, I've implemented a lot of these practices, put them to the test, and collected only the most effective ones in my toolbox. I've come up with my own ideas on how to set and achieve big goals. I've eliminated the ineffective, amped up the effective, and put it all together in a system that works.

This is a photo of me from 2012. I was morbidly obese, weighing in at 138 kilograms (304 pounds). I worked sixty- to eighty-hour workweeks and rarely took the weekends off. The photo of my daughter Leiah and me was taken in my office when my wife brought her over to see me one weekend. That's how M.I.A. I was at home. I ran an insurance brokerage at the time, and by then, the money was good, but everything else in life had been put on the back burner to achieve those financial goals. I didn't look like the kind of guy who worked out or reached for a salad for lunch, and rightly so. I did not. I lived on caffeine and fast food.

It was around this time that I also decided to get all my personal financial affairs in order. First port of call: My Life Insurance policy needed an upgrade. A lot of new parents feel a sense of urgency to get their finances sorted when their 'heirs' make an appearance, and I felt it, too, when my daughter was born. So, I approached the Life Insurance companies that I had worked with for so long, for whom I had generated millions worth of sales, and asked them for a quote for some additional life insurance coverage for myself. I had some in place before this point, but nothing that had needed me to undergo medical tests.

This time, I did need to undergo those medicals. Upon reviewing my medical reports, the insurers came back to me with a quote that made my jaw drop: It was a whopping 100 percent higher than the average individual my age. Why? They didn't hold back when they answered. They told me that, given my current weight and lifestyle, they didn't expect me to live past the policy expiration date. In other words, they didn't expect me to live past age 69. They expected to have to pay out the proceeds of my policy to my family because I was likely to succumb to a lifestyle disease, heart failure, or something else along those lines and drop dead before I hit age 69.

Yikes.

It was the wake-up call I needed. Over the next few months, I started to chart out the best way for me to reverse the damage my lifestyle had caused. After consulting several doctors and well-being experts, we identified that the first step was drastic weight loss. The path I chose was extreme: A bariatric sleeve surgery. The surgery involves removing a part of the stomach and leaving behind only a narrow 'sleeve' of the organ. The reduced stomach size dramatically reduces appetite, hunger signals, and your overall ability to eat much food. Like I said: Extreme, but in my case, effective.

Over the next six months, I lost over 45 kilos. I started to exercise alongside the post-surgery weight loss. At first, three times a week at home with a personal trainer. As I started to get fitter and wanted to challenge myself more, I stumbled upon the world of CrossFit, and from there, I discovered the world of ultramarathons.

I've always been attracted to larger-than-life, seemingly impossible goals. And so, a lot about this ultra-fitness space drew me in.

And then, a couple of events changed the trajectory of my life and career. On December 31, 2016, I exited two business partnerships on the same day—one through a hostile takeover, and the other due to a values and compatibility mismatch. What's more, I found myself facing a little over $550,000 worth of debt to my name. Over the next couple of years, that debt ballooned to $2 million. How I got there is a story for another time, but it was a combination of poor decisions and consequent actions, both mine and those of the other people involved.

As with most turbulence in our lives, this crisis came at an inconvenient time. We were a young couple, with two kids in tow, our parents were growing old and needed support, and just when I needed my financial house in order, it was falling apart. It wasn't just falling apart; there was also a great big sinkhole under it in the form of debt. I knew I had only one option: take charge of this narrative and flip it.

And so, I did.

At the time, I sold life insurance and medical insurance, earning between $45,000 and $50,000 in monthly commissions. That wasn't going to cut it anymore. I needed to pay $12,500 every month just towards servicing the interest on my debt, but I didn't want to be chipping away at this debt for the rest of my life. I wanted to pay it down in big chunks, close it, and move on. There were also the day-to-day expenses to be covered by that paycheck.

There were two ways for me to boost my income:

- Sell more policies to more people (sales volume), OR
- Sell larger policies (size of transaction).

Parallel to this eye-opener, I had also been closely observing the top performers at MDRT—the individuals at the Top of the Table (TOT) level—and learned that their growth didn't necessarily come from selling more. Many of them made it to that table by selling 'big.'

It was when these realisations collided that it became very clear to me: my way forward was to master the large-value life insurance space and the high-net-worth (HNW) and ultra-high-net-worth (UHNW) clients who needed it.

So, I picked that lane. Ever since, I've made it my core focus to understand and serve that market to my fullest capability. Today, my team and I are responsible for $1 billion worth of life coverage. I've paid the debt off and am on to bigger, more energising goals.

I'm not here to tell you that large-value life insurance or HNW clients are your path to success. That might be so, but that is not what I want you to take back from this book.

What I want you to take back is this: There is immense power, clarity, and focus that comes from identifying your niche market, committing to one game, getting to know your playing field, and then locking your eyes on your goalpost.

In my experience, the moment you cut out the noise and distractions, swap short-term gains for long-term wins, and choose to become a true master of your craft, you will surpass your wildest dreams.

I hope that, over the course of this book, I can give you the blueprint for exactly how to do that.

1

TAKING CONTROL—
YOUR FUTURE IS IN YOUR HANDS

Success is not an accident. Not in my world, nor in the world you chose to step into when you picked up a copy of this book.

People seem to only see the tip of the iceberg: the end result, the glory, the wins. They often miss everything beneath the surface: the hard work, sleepless nights, sacrifices, and strategic decisions that led to that outcome. The same principle applies to building the life and career you want.

But you're here, and that tells me something important. You're ready. You want more. And not just more in the sense of a higher paycheck—although that's part of it—but more in terms of impact, freedom, and fulfilment. You want to feel alive and in control, not just in your career but in every aspect of your life. Perhaps you've already achieved some level of success, but now you're hungry for exponential growth. You're not here to maintain the status quo. You're here to shatter limits and redefine what's possible.

Let's come to terms with something first: It's not going to be easy. You've probably read books and attended seminars that promised quick-fix solutions or a magic bullet to get ahead. This isn't one of those books. This is a guide built on the real-world, battle-tested principles that I've used to transform my career and my entire life. I'm not going to sugarcoat things or offer you shortcuts. Instead, I'll show you how to take complete control over every aspect of your journey.

Taking 'control' doesn't just mean dictating the pace or choosing your own path. It means accepting full responsibility for your life and your results. The acronym C.O.N.T.R.O.L. stands for the seven foundational pillars that will help you set and achieve game-changing, life-changing goals.

Clear Goals: You need to know what you're aiming for. Clarity drives results. If you don't have a clear destination in mind, you're just spinning your wheels. I'll show you how to set motivating and achievable targets.

Ownership: No one is coming to save you. But there are people out there who can and will help you. Ownership means holding yourself accountable, not doing this on your own. It means not having anyone or anything to 'blame' for your outcomes and results. It means controlling what you can control: Your response, your mindset, your actions, rather than everything beyond you.

Know Your **N**umbers: The data never lies. I'm going to ask you to do the uncomfortable work of getting to know your numbers inside and out—whether it's your sales metrics or your personal finances. Numbers will give you the feedback you need to adjust and improve. It's ironic how many financial advisors – the 'numbers people' – shy away from their own numbers.

Tactics: Strategies are essential. The right strategy can be game-changing. However, even the best strategy is useless without the right tactics. These are the day-to-day moves, the 'reps' you put in to move towards your goal. Once you have a game plan, you need tactical execution. I'll break down all my best and most relevant tactics for you. It is your job to go out and execute.

Right-Fit Clients: Not all clients are created equal. The key to scaling your business is serving clients who align with your goals and values. I'll show you how to identify and attract your ideal clients—those who will help you grow, not just survive. This concept was something I learned from Dan Sullivan, Co-Founder of Strategic Coach®.

Obsession: Ordinary effort yields ordinary results. If you want extraordinary outcomes, you need to be obsessed with your craft. I'll help you find that fire within, the drive to keep pushing when most people would quit.

Life: This journey isn't just about your career. It's about building a life you love. Financial success without personal fulfilment is hollow. In this final section, I'll guide you on how to integrate your professional ambitions with the rest of your life so you can have it all.

Before we dive into these pillars and how you can implement each one in your business and life, let's take a moment to get into the right headspace.

HOW HIGH-PERFORMERS THINK

You're probably familiar with the saying, "The harder I work, the luckier I get." There's a reason this rings true. Success comes to those who consistently put in the work, who show up every day with a relentless determination to improve. I'm a big believer in working smart and optimising effort rather than just grinding away mindlessly. Intentionality and work aligned with a goal-informed plan will carry you much farther than just 'hard work.'

High performers don't leave their lives to chance. They take control of every aspect—from setting their goals to executing them to optimising their time and energy. And above all, they never settle for mediocrity. They know that they can always do more, be more, and give more.

As we go through each of the steps in the Take C.O.N.T.R.O.L Model^{TP}, you'll notice a recurring theme: It all starts and ends with you. The external factors don't matter as much as the environment you create within and directly around you. I've seen advisors in the worst markets, and economies thrive because they didn't let circumstances dictate their results. Conversely, I've seen advisors in booming economies fall flat because they let external conditions lull them into complacency.

This framework is about eliminating that complacency. It's about teaching you how to cultivate a mindset where challenges become opportunities, failures are just stepping stones, and every setback fuels your next breakthrough.

THE ROAD AHEAD

In my 25 years in the life insurance industry (as of the writing of this book), I've gone through ups and downs, personal and professional wins and losses. I've made a lot of mistakes, but I've also learned invaluable lessons along the way. The Take C.O.N.T.R.O.L Model is the result of those hard-earned lessons.

The path to mastery in this or any industry requires more than just knowledge. It requires discipline, focus, and a willingness to do what others won't. Whether you're just starting out or you've been in the game for years, the principles in this book will challenge you to think differently, act with intention, and break through whatever is holding you back.

I'm not going to pretend it's a quick fix or an overnight transformation. Real change takes time, but the rewards are worth every ounce of effort. I know this because I've lived it. Today, my life is a testament to the power of taking control. And it all started with these principles.

So, as you move forward through this book, I challenge you to do something important: Don't just read. Reflect. Absorb. And most importantly, act. This is not a spectator sport. Or rather, it might be for people watching you do your thing. But you are the player in the arena. This is your game. The question is: Are you ready to take control?

$$2$$

CLEAR, MEANINGFUL GOALS— THE FOUNDATION OF SUCCESS

Setting goals is the first step to turning the invisible into the visible.

—Tony Robbins

It's June 2007. I'm making my way to my first-ever Million Dollar Round Table (MDRT) Annual Meeting. This was the fourth time I had qualified for MDRT, but the first time I had planned for and was able to afford the trip to North America to attend the meeting. The meeting that year was to be hosted in Denver, Colorado, and incidentally, it would be my first trip over the Atlantic Ocean.

That also meant it was the first time I was going to be in the vicinity of my wife's hometown, Toronto, Canada. So we decided to make what the kids call a 'work-cation' out of it. We planned to go to Denver first, attend MDRT, and then take a three-week vacation in Toronto.

The challenge? While MDRT required me to reach $99,000 in commissions to qualify, that $99,000 was not going to cover our personal expenses that year, which now included a month-long trip to North America. And, of course, as a financial advisor who earns his paychecks as a result of meeting clients and closing sales, that month-long MDRT/vacation period was also going to be a zero-revenue period for me. But we'd still need to make rent, pay our car loans, and other recurring living expenses in Dubai during that period.

I crunched some numbers and worked out that I needed to generate $195,000 for the year to be comfortable—nearly double the MDRT requirement. So, I set to work to hit that goal.

I wish I knew half the things I'm going to share with you in the next few pages back then. It would have been much easier to hit that goal. But with a can-do attitude, I did my best, and I did hit the goal. I surpassed it, in fact, and closed the year at $210,000. My point?

Well, I've got a few points to make here, so I'll break them down.

1. THE GOAL PROVIDES DIRECTION

Imagine a ship setting sail without a destination. No matter how well-built or fast it is, without a clear course, it will drift aimlessly, at the mercy of the tides and winds. The same principle applies to your life and career. If you don't set a destination, you'll find yourself drifting without direction, reacting to whatever comes your way. I call this the Directional Goal Principle[IP].

This isn't just an inspiring metaphor; it's a powerful one. The science of goal-setting strongly supports this idea. Dr Edwin Locke's Goal-Setting Theory, developed in the 1960s, demonstrates that clear and challenging goals have a significant impact on improving performance. Locke's research, conducted in collaboration with Gary Latham, revealed that specific and challenging goals lead to better results than vague or easy ones.[1] Clear goals give you focus and make it easier to measure progress. When you know where you're headed, you can direct your energy toward meaningful actions and course-correct along the way.

Furthermore, achieving small milestones releases dopamine in your brain, reinforcing your motivation and creating a positive feedback loop. It's this sense of achievement that propels you forward toward bigger and bigger wins.

Books like *Atomic Habits* by James Clear also emphasise how even small actions, when performed consistently, can lead to massive results. While goals provide the destination, it's your day-to-day habits—the systems you create—that help you reach that destination. This concept will be explored further in this chapter, but the main takeaway is that goals alone aren't enough; they need to be broken down into manageable steps that build momentum.

If I had just looked at that number, $195,000, I would have shaken my head and said it was impossible. But I decided to just focus on the bite-sized goal. Assuming I needed 100 clients at $1,950 in commission each, I focused on securing that next client meeting, that next 'yes.' The key is to chip away at the block slowly.

In the same way, if you told Rickson 1.0—obese, workaholic, caffeine-and fast-food-fuelled Rickson—that he was to drop half his body weight and run 237 kilometres across the Sahara Desert, the guy would have laughed in your face! But it was gradual: one step at a time.

First, I had a Bariatric Sleeve surgery, and then the weight began to disappear without my doing very much. Believe me, the sleeve did not turn me into someone who loved exercise... or wanted to run long distances across the desert. But then people started complimenting me on my weight loss, and my clothes started fitting better. I started to look and feel better. I started exercising a little bit, and I got more positive results and reinforcement. Now, people started to notice how 'fit' I was starting to look. More positive results; more reinforcement. That not-so-vicious cycle created a total lifestyle shift for me.

What I'm getting at is this: It doesn't all have to be one big leap. Don't underestimate the power of those first few small shifts.

2. WHEN YOUR INCOME IS 'UP TO YOU,' YOU NEED GOALS MORE THAN ANYONE ELSE!

If you're in a commission-based profession, like most financial advisors are, your success depends entirely on the results you generate. You don't have the security of a fixed salary, which makes the need for clear goals even more critical. Without them, you risk drifting from month to month, struggling to make ends meet. That uncertainty is difficult and manifests as desperation, negativity, and other negative energies that show up when you're in front of a prospect.

I'm going to digress here to share a quick story with you. When I first started out in the business, I still lived at home with my parents. I had no rent, no utility bills, and a fully paid Toyota Corolla. My monthly expenses were under AED 2,500 (~$680). One commission check could cover two months of my out-of-pocket expenses. I didn't *need* to push harder, and that was the problem. There was no urgency. There was no 'next step' or direction in which I was moving.

That's when I decided to shake things up. I wanted more. I wanted a better car. I wanted the independence of my own space. So, I financed a Nissan Pathfinder and moved into a studio apartment. My fixed monthly expenses jumped by over AED 3,000 (~$815) overnight. It was a conscious decision to increase the pressure. I put myself in a position where I *had* to sell more to sustain the lifestyle I wanted. That shift changed everything. Bigger responsibilities demanded bigger results. Once I raised the bar in my life, I had no choice but to raise the bar in my performance.

A lot of the principles that you will come across when you model and study the work of successful financial advisors will boil down to ideas like 'Having a long-term mindset,' 'Building trust and solid client relationships without pushing for a sale,' and more. But these things take time. It's hard to 'slow down' and time the right moment to pitch when you need the commission from a sale to pay your outstanding bills.

This is the Income Clarity Law[IP]. For you and me, goals are much more than just a nice-to-have motivator. They are a necessity for us to be able to operate with integrity and in the best interest of our clients.

3. SETTING NON-ARBITRARY GOALS

When your goals are personally meaningful, they become more than just targets—they become your internal compass, guiding you through challenges and helping you stay the course.

Arbitrary goals often lack emotional weight. When your goals are not tied to something you genuinely care about, they lose their power to motivate you during tough times. On the other hand, when your goals align with your core values, they give you the strength to keep going, no matter the obstacles.

For me, goal-setting has been at the core of both my professional achievements and personal growth. Clear, meaningful goals are the driving force behind everything I do. These aren't arbitrary targets but goals tied to things that matter to me deeply—whether it's achieving financial freedom, providing for my family, or serving my clients with excellence.

Goals like "I want to make $10,000 this month" or "I want to close five deals" are often too superficial. They might give you a short-term target, but if they lack personal meaning, they won't keep you motivated for long. Goals need to go beyond surface-level desires. They must reflect something deeper—a desire to build a life of meaning, impact, and purpose.

So, how do you ensure your goals are non-arbitrary and personally meaningful?

Here is the 3-Step Goal Setting Formula[IP]—your guide to setting goals that resonate deeply with you.

STEP 1: START WITH YOUR 'WHY'

Before setting any goal, ask yourself why it matters. What's driving you to achieve it? Is it the desire for financial freedom? The need to create a legacy? A commitment to personal growth? What do these results – being financially free, having a legacy, experiencing personal growth – mean to you, and how do they directly impact and change your life and the lives of your loved ones?

Without a clear 'why,' your goals will lack the emotional depth needed to keep you committed when things get tough. For instance, setting a goal to earn more money without understanding why it's important to you won't cut it when the going gets tough. However, if your goal is to earn more because it will provide stability for your family or give you the freedom to pursue your true passion, such as the financial and time freedom, it would mean you could finally set up that restaurant that serves up only your late grandmother's recipes… now that's a much stronger motivator.

I've found that the more personal and connected to my values my goals are, the more committed I am to achieving them. The goals aren't just about hitting a number—they're about what that number represents for my life and the people I care about.

STEP 2: MAKE YOUR GOALS SPECIFIC

Once you've identified your 'why,' you need to make your goals specific and clear. Vague goals like "I want to be successful" or "I want to make more money" aren't enough. You need to be clear about what success looks like for you.

For example, instead of setting a generic goal like "I want to increase my income," make it personal and specific: "I want to close three high-value policies by the end of this quarter, with a total of $50,000 in commissions, to add to our savings and take the family on vacation this year." This goal isn't just a number—it's tied to something meaningful that motivates you on a deeper level.

I also like to follow the SMART Objectives framework, as dated as it might be. SMART in the world of goal-setting stands for:

Specific
Measurable
Achievable
Realistic (I prefer Relevant)
Time-bound

The goal I've spelt out above checks all the boxes.

Specific: 'I want to close three high-value policies this quarter, with a total of $50,000 in commissions'

Measurable: Three deals, $50,000 in commissions—that's an objective measure!

Achievable: Assuming I have potential clients who are likely to purchase policies of this size in a pipeline, this goal might be achievable. Otherwise, I'd need to figure out HOW exactly to achieve this goal. I do not believe that your current circumstances dictate what is possible for your future; this is more a checkpoint or a data point than a reality that you cannot change.

Relevant: Personal relevance. As a result of achieving these numbers, I want to take my family on a well-deserved holiday. That feels personal and relevant to me! This isn't *just* to hit some target I've been given by a manager.

Time-bound: The goal states 'by the end of this quarter'—you could put down a date if you like. If this were the last quarter of the year, for instance, and you know that most of your clients will plug out by mid-December for the holiday season, consider your cut-off to hit the goal on December 1st. Our team's cut-off is November 30th.

STEP 3: BREAK DOWN BIG GOALS INTO ACTIONABLE STEPS

Big goals can be overwhelming. The key to achieving large goals is breaking them down into smaller, actionable steps.

While long-term goals give you direction, short-term goals provide a sense of progress and reassurance—you've got this. These smaller steps are crucial in building momentum and keeping you on track.

For instance, if your long-term goal is to close $250,000 in commissions this year, break it down into smaller, manageable targets. How many clients do you need to meet with each week? How many calls or meetings should you schedule daily? What should the minimum check be, and what is the largest check that you are currently working on? What are your daily, weekly, and monthly goals?

By focusing on these smaller, short-term goals and documenting them, you'll make consistent progress toward your larger objective without feeling overwhelmed and without getting lost in the 'bigness' of the vision.

Breaking down big goals into actionable steps has helped me achieve some seemingly impossible goals. Like going from not even being able to run 10 kilometres (~6 miles) to running 237 kilometres (~147 miles) across the Sahara desert with six months of training. Or jumping from producing 7x Top of the Table numbers in 2022 to producing 12x Top of the Table numbers in 2023.

Whether personal goals or goals I set with my team, I only achieved each of these massive, seemingly impossible goals by breaking them down into smaller, actionable steps that I could take today. Steps that were largely in my control. I must say here: The outcome of taking this action was NOT the part I could control.

I couldn't (still can't, and never will be able to) 'make' a client buy. What I could control was the number of prospects I reached out to every day. What I could control was the number of meetings I had booked on my calendar every week. What I could do was master my subject and product, and learn everything I could about my client, so that I showed up with the most powerful sales and service proposition possible. As a result? I could simply influence my chances of closing the deal and hitting my goals. It is key to remember that the Take Control Framework[IP] is about taking control of your actions, your mindset, and your approach. It is not about 'controlling' or attempting to control anyone else's actions.

Back to breaking your goals down: It's something that has become second nature to me now, just as it will to you as you apply this strategy. Instead of fixating on one massive target, I focus on what I need to do each day or week. This keeps me grounded and allows me to celebrate smaller wins along the way, too. The smaller win is not just a smaller case closed along the way. I also take the time to celebrate indicators that I am on the right track. Like getting introduced to a right-fit client, whether or not business is on the table today. Or like seeing that my pipeline of business waiting to happen is bigger than the business I have closed so far.

LONG-TERM AND SHORT-TERM GOALS: STRIKING THE BALANCE

Long-term goals give you purpose, but without short-term goals, those far-away goals feel distant and perhaps even unachievable. You need both long-term and short-term goals to succeed.

Long-term goals represent your big vision: The destination toward which you're steering your ship. Short-term goals are the milestones that keep you moving forward. Think of the short-term goals as 'Rest Stops' on your long journey—they're great points for you to realign with the vision, refuel, and re-stock provisions. They give you the satisfaction of progress, ensuring that you're consistently taking steps toward your ultimate goal.

In my journey, balancing long-term vision with short-term execution has been critical. I always have a clear idea of where I want to go in the long run, but I stay focused on the daily actions that are relevant to only me – unapologetically.

To demonstrate this, I am going to share with you how I approached training for my ultramarathon across the Sahara Desert. Signing up for the Marathon des Sables (MDS) meant that I had under six months to go from being a beginner runner to being able to run 237 kilometres (~147 miles) across the Moroccan Sahara Desert.

When I first heard about MDS, it wasn't an instant 'goal' that I locked in on. I had attended an informal talk at the gym, where some of the guys had gone and done MDS and came back to share their experience. It sounded intense. I was intrigued, but that was about it. I went on about my CrossFit training as usual, without really thinking about this mammoth race.

One day, I ran into Omar and Jimmy, a couple of friends I hadn't seen in weeks, at the gym. Both had lost a ton of weight and dropped a whole lot of muscle. Frankly, they looked like they'd been through a bit of an ordeal… And they had. They'd both just completed MDS. And when he told me the stories—being on drips, collapsing mid-race, crawling their way through parts of it—I was both shocked and weirdly inspired.

That night, I got into a full-blown argument with my wife, Sangeeta, about the idea of my doing something this extreme. And then I did what every stubborn man does after a fight: I Googled the race and decided I wanted to do it.

I did not start with a plan. I didn't even speak to my coach, Marcus, who would later be one of the most powerful forces in my training regimen. I just started running. Weekends, mostly. A few kilometres here, a few more there. In about five weeks, I went from running zero kilometres to knocking out twenty-eight kilometres in one go. That kind of running without the right training plan to support it wasn't a good idea… I had shin splints and all kinds of issues. I realised there was no way I was going to be able to just 'run' my way to that finish line. I needed training and guidance from someone who had done this kind of thing before. So I reached out to Marcus, my coach at my CrossFit box, for help.

I told him I was serious about training for MDS. His response was simple: "Then sign up."

You see, I'd mentally committed to doing the race, but it was only that official act of registering that moved this from "something cool I'd like to do" to "something I am doing." Goals don't become real until you put something on the line.

From there, the training became a process of layers, exactly the same way you need to layer up your own growth goals. First, we built basic running endurance. I went from three runs a week to four. One of those was always a long run on the weekend. Then we started pushing the distances. Then we changed the timing of the runs. I started running later in the day, so I could get used to the heat. Eventually, we added trail running and then desert running.

At the same time, I had to dial down my CrossFit sessions. I learned the hard way that recovery is a training strategy in itself. I had to learn how to rest, refuel, and eat for this kind of sustained effort. My diet changed, too. More carbs, more energy-dense foods. Eventually, I began practising eating and sleeping the way I would on the race. I'd eat dehydrated meals, camp out in a sleeping bag on my bedroom floor (while my wife slept on the bed!) just to simulate what race week would feel like.

And then there was the mental side of the training. That's the part no one prepares you for. Marcus would have me park at the edge of the desert, pick a single sand dune, and run up and down it for three or four hours straight. Not a loop. Not a trail. One sand dune. Over and over again.

It was mind-numbing. But that was the point. "During the race," Marcus told me, "you're going to want to quit. This is how you build the mindset that won't let you." He was right. Eventually, I was doing back-to-back desert runs: running for three or four hours on a Friday, camping overnight, waking up to run for eight hours across the desert solo, navigating by map, then returning, eating, resting, and going back out to run again. Then sleep in the desert again and run the next day before coming home.

In addition to this, I started joining local trail races, ranging from 15K to 35K runs on unfamiliar trails and terrains, so I could get my body used to the unexpected and also get used to being part of a running community. Every small shift made a big difference. Shoes, gear, nutrition, sleep, hydration—everything had to be thought through, tested, and adapted. And every decision, every run, every sand dune climbed was a tiny piece of the big goal falling into place.

That's what it takes.

Whether your goal is to cross a finish line in the desert, qualify for MDRT, or hit your first $250,000 year, the path is the same: Break it down. Test it. Commit fully. Then chip away at it one step, one decision, one day at a time.

SIDEBAR: THE 'MEANINGFUL' BIT WITH MY MDS GOAL

Looking back, the decision to run MDS wasn't really about the race. It was about taking back my power.

At the time, I had just come out of two business partnerships that had gone completely south. I had exited both partnerships on the same day and was staring down over half a million dollars in debt. It was one of the lowest points of my life. Everything felt like it was spiralling, and the worst part was the sense that I no longer had control of my own story.

Running MDS was my way of flipping that narrative. It was a way of proving to myself that I still had agency. That I could still choose a goal so audacious, so ridiculous, that it would demand the best of me, and that I could rise to meet it.

When you're in a tough spot, personally, professionally, or financially, there's a lot that can feel outside your control. But the one thing you can always choose is your response. MDS became mine. It was the reset I needed. A new challenge, on my terms. And by the time I crossed that finish line in the desert, it had become much more than a finisher's medal for me. Crossing that finishing line was about reclaiming the pen and writing the next chapter of my life with power, intention, and self-respect.

THE TL;DR VERSION

If your income is up to you, then your goals are your GPS. Without them, you're just drifting from one month to the next, reacting instead of creating.

Clear, meaningful goals give you direction, purpose, and fuel. They stop you from making decisions out of desperation and help you operate from a place of intention and integrity.

But goals only work when they're specific, personal, and broken down into actionable steps. Vague goals like "earn more money" or "be successful" won't cut it. You need goals that are tied to your 'why'— goals that actually mean something to you. Then, you need to break them down into bite-sized pieces that you can execute daily.

This is how I went from being unable to run 10 kilometres to completing 237 kilometres across the Sahara Desert. Not overnight. Not by magic. But by taking one step at a time and building consistency, endurance, and mindset over months of training.

The same principle applies to any goal—income, fitness, impact, or freedom.

The secret is the Commit-Then-Build Philosophy[IP]: Don't wait until the goal feels doable. Commit first. Break it down. Build your system. And move.

Every big result is just the compound interest of small steps taken consistently.

3

OWNERSHIP—YOUR ACTIONS, YOUR RESULTS

Until you take ownership of your life, you will always be a victim.

—Steve Maraboli

In the summer of 2024, my wife and I travelled to Europe with our two kids. We spent a total of 43 days there, visiting over 21 cities and towns during the holiday. One of our favourites from the trip was a charming town called Setúbal, Portugal, where we met Miguel.

Miguel and his wife, Paula, took us on eBike tours across Setúbal. After successfully selling and exiting their hotel business, they started this and a few other businesses, including a hiking tours company and an events management company.

Miguel worked hard. He chose not to be the wealth-building CEO he could have been. He decided not to expand his hotel into a chain and sit back and reap the rewards. Because his version of wealth was different. His version of wealth was enjoying freedom of time and the chance to move his body every day. (The guy bikes over 200 kilometres a day owing to the bike tours he guides!)

Could Miguel live the life of a king if he wanted to? Probably. He's enterprising, has business experience, and has all the building blocks to turn his business into an empire. But he didn't want that. He wanted a simple life. And he chose a simple life, with all the good and the not-so-good that comes with that.

In Miguel's absolute joy with the life he had built, I saw one thing: ownership. He had chosen a path and owned all the pleasures and consequences that came with it.

That afternoon, I had a long chat with my kids about taking ownership of the consequences and results of their life decisions. At 14 and 11, they kept switching between being captivated by the conversation and picking the next track on Spotify, but I think we made some core memory material there. And even if they were just the ramblings of their old man to the kids, that glimpse into Miguel's life definitely made me think about the role taking ownership plays in living a life of abundance.

Ownership is the bedrock for growth. In the world of financial services, particularly where you are solely responsible for the results you create, you will find it easier to lean into excuses and reasons not to achieve your goal if you do not ground yourself in a strong sense of ownership. You'll see the obstacles and things outside your control as justifiable reasons not to take the steps to create the results you want.

You've chosen a line of work that is essentially entrepreneurial. The stakes are clear: Your success is directly tied to your ability to take control of your business, your relationships with clients, and ultimately, your income.

In this chapter, we'll look at the importance of ownership from a financial advisor's perspective, drawing lessons from real-world experiences and insights from thought leaders who understand the transformative power of self-accountability.

OWNERSHIP IN A COMMISSION-BASED CAREER

As a financial advisor, your career is performance-driven. You don't have the luxury of a fixed salary; every dollar you earn directly reflects your ability to close deals, serve clients, and grow your income. Ownership is not just a nice-to-have, 'ideal-world' personal philosophy; it's necessary for survival and success.

In a commission-based career, it's easy to blame external factors when things don't go your way. The market may be slow, or your leads have dried up. Perhaps clients aren't ready to commit, or you're not getting the referrals you expected. But here's the hard truth: Every challenge you face in your business is an opportunity to take ownership.

When I first aimed for MDRT qualification, I quickly learned that the difference between success and failure was directly tied to my ability to take full responsibility for my results. Instead of blaming the market, the recession, or whatever other circumstances outside of my control, I asked myself: 'What can I do here to make this work for me? What can I do to ensure I stay on track to achieve my goals?' This shift in mindset allowed me to see the gaps in my strategy, refine my approach, and ultimately scale my income—something I now incorporate as a regular reflection exercise.

THE PSYCHOLOGY OF OWNERSHIP

Ownership goes beyond taking responsibility for sales numbers. It's about taking ownership of every interaction you have with clients, prospects, and even yourself. Studies on self-determination and human behaviour reveal a direct link between ownership and personal empowerment.[2]

Edward Deci and Richard Ryan, pioneers of the self-determination theory, argue that people have three basic psychological needs: autonomy, competence, and relatedness. Autonomy, the ability to control one's own actions and outcomes, is foundational to personal growth and fulfilment.[3]

As a financial advisor, while this varies from organisation to organisation, it is safe to say that you enjoy more autonomy than most professionals. For the most part, you control your time, client relationships, and strategies to earn an income. When you take ownership of these elements, you tap into that sense of autonomy. You're no longer dependent on external validation or outcomes dictated by others.

Instead, you are the architect of your own success. Your game, your rules.

This is crucial for long-term satisfaction and growth, both professionally and personally. When you take ownership of your actions and decisions, you gain the ability to shape your results in a way that most salaried professionals cannot.

THE OPPOSITE OF OWNERSHIP: VICTIMHOOD IN FINANCIAL ADVISORY

Let's take a moment here to talk about the flip side of the ownership coin: Blame Culture. It's tempting to blame external factors for your failures or lack of progress—the fluctuating market, high competition, or even the nature of your prospects. The financial advisory world can be unpredictable, but when you shift the blame and make it about something you cannot control, you relinquish your ability to shape your career and future. The second you say, "It's the market," you've given up your ability to influence the outcome.

Authors Jocko Willink and Leif Babin, in their book *Extreme Ownership*, emphasise that leaders who take full responsibility for everything within their control ultimately create the conditions for success.[4] Their principle, "There are no bad teams, only bad leaders," underscores the value of extreme accountability. In the context of financial advisors, I'd go so far as to say, "There are no bad markets, only bad strategies."

'Blaming' the market, the lack of training you've received, or even your clients' slow response times all make you a victim of these circumstances. They limit your potential to grow because your message to yourself is, 'I can't do anything about this.' But when you decide to own your results, no matter the circumstances, you empower yourself to shift the narrative, find solutions, and achieve the success you're aiming for, whether that's making it to MDRT this year or shedding fifty pounds and reversing that diabetes diagnosis.

OWNERSHIP OF YOUR THOUGHTS: YOUR MINDSET IS YOUR GREATEST ASSET

Every decision, every interaction, and every signed contract starts in one place: Your thoughts. These thoughts become beliefs, and your beliefs shape how you perceive the world, your clients, and your potential.

In *Mindset: The New Psychology of Success*, Carol Dweck differentiates between a fixed mindset and a growth mindset.[5] Advisors with a fixed mindset believe their talent is static—they blame external circumstances for their shortcomings and see challenges as threats. However, those with a growth mindset take ownership of their thoughts, seeing challenges as opportunities for learning and improvement.

When pursuing MDRT or any high-level financial goals, you must first master your mindset. Instead of saying, "This is too difficult; the target is too high," challenge yourself to think, "What can I learn? How can I improve my approach?"

When you own your thoughts, you'll notice a dramatic shift in how you approach client meetings, structure your time, and pursue large commissions. By controlling your internal dialogue, you can shift from merely surviving in your career to thriving.

OWNERSHIP OF YOUR ACTIONS: BUILDING CONSISTENCY IN FINANCIAL ADVISORY

James Clear, author of *Atomic Habits*, shares something in his book that has stuck with me since I first read it: "We are what we repeatedly do."[6]

Think about it: What do you repeatedly find yourself doing? Your success depends on consistent action: making the calls, following up with leads, nurturing client relationships, and refining your sales skills. These are not one-time efforts but habits that compound over time.

Taking ownership of your actions means recognising that the daily grind—the calls, the meetings, the presentations—builds your business and income. Back in the day, when I was just getting started as a Financial Advisor, I had the good fortune of being mentored by one of the best advisors in the business. He introduced me to '10-3-1': Make 10 calls a day, meet three prospects, and attempt to close one deal daily. Was it a challenge to hit those goals? Yes.

But they set the bar high enough that it was hard NOT to be selling or learning how to sell better as a result!

It's easy to overlook small tasks, but as Clear explains, habits are the compound interest of self-improvement. Every extra call you make, every follow-up you pursue, builds momentum.

If you want to reach MDRT or even Top of the Table status, your actions must be consistent. Are you tracking your daily performance? Are you setting targets for the number of calls, client meetings, and policies that you close? It is hard to create exponential growth and results by chance. It is unlikely that you'll stumble your way to a six-figure income or just wake up to find that you've hit the qualifying criteria one morning. This is going to take mindful, consistent action, even when you don't feel like it and even when things do not seem to be going your way. Commit to this one piece; the whole journey will feel that much easier.

OWNERSHIP OF YOUR RESULTS: SUCCESS AND FAILURE IN ACHIEVING MDRT

One of the toughest aspects of ownership is taking responsibility for your failures. In a commission-based industry, failure can feel personal. Perhaps you didn't close as many deals as you'd hoped or fell short of your annual income target. It's tempting to look for reasons outside yourself, but as John C. Maxwell points out in his book *Failing Forward*, failure is simply an opportunity to learn.[7] Not achieving your goals is merely a data point.

I encountered multiple setbacks when I first set out to qualify for MDRT. Some clients backed out at the last minute, while others didn't purchase the large policies I had hoped for. My biggest wake-up calls came when I made mistakes—sold something wrong to a client or overlooked a crucial detail that affected the payouts to their family. These were crushing moments for me. However, every failure was an opportunity to review my process. What could I do differently? What did I need to learn from this experience? How could I drastically reduce the odds of it happening again?

When you own the consequences of your actions—whether success or failure—you unlock a deep sense of responsibility and self-respect. The greatest, most successful people aren't people who have made no mistakes or experienced no failures. They are the people who stood up again, dusted off, and kept going. Instead of letting setbacks define you, use them as a stepping stone to propel you toward your goals.

This seems like an apt place to insert one of my favourite quotes attributed to Muhammad Ali of all time:

"You don't lose when you get knocked down. You lose when you stay down."

OWNERSHIP PROTOCOL[IP]: ACTIONABLE STEPS FOR TAKING OWNERSHIP IN YOUR FINANCIAL ADVISORY CAREER

1. IDENTIFY AREAS WHERE YOU LACK OWNERSHIP

Look at your sales numbers, client relationships, and business strategy. Are there areas where you've been placing blame or avoiding responsibility? Is it in your follow-up process? Your prospecting strategy? Once identified, commit to taking full responsibility and taking action to improve.

2. TRACK YOUR KEY METRICS

As a financial advisor, numbers don't lie. Start tracking key performance metrics, like daily calls made, client meetings, policies closed, and total commissions. How many calls did it take to close one deal in 2024? What does that look like in 2025? Has the metric improved? This level of ownership over your actions will give you the clarity to consistently improve and grow.

3. USE FAILURES AS LEARNING OPPORTUNITIES

Every setback is an opportunity to improve your approach. Instead of focusing on what went wrong, ask yourself, "What can I learn from this?" and "How can I do better next time?" By owning your failures, you set yourself up for future success.

4. CELEBRATE YOUR WINS—BIG OR SMALL

Ownership isn't just about handling failure; it's also about celebrating your wins. Every time you close a deal, hit a sales target, or get closer to MDRT qualification, take a moment to acknowledge your hard work and success. This reinforces the power of ownership and builds confidence for future challenges.

By taking ownership of your thoughts, actions, and outcomes, you move from being reactive to being proactive in your career. Whether your goal is to qualify for MDRT or simply double your income as a stepping stone towards that goal, ownership is the key to unlocking that next level. You are in control of your future—now it's time to take the reins into your hands.

THE TL;DR VERSION

In the financial services industry, your success is directly tied to your ability to take ownership of your outcomes. Excuses might feel valid. It's easy to blame the market, your clients, or external circumstances. But here's the reality: those are just distractions from the real work. It will feel like a frustrating, uphill battle until you take full responsibility for your results and start focusing on the things you can change, improve, and take control of.

Being a financial advisor is an entrepreneurial role. You don't get the safety net of a fixed salary. You're responsible for every commission you earn, every deal you close, and every client relationship you build. Taking ownership means facing the reality of a situation, no matter how difficult, and asking yourself, "What can I do that is within my control to achieve my goals?"

You have more autonomy than most professionals. Use it. Taking ownership puts you in the driver's seat of your career, allowing you to control your future. Blame nothing and no one. The sooner you get to 'I am responsible for all my successes and failures,' the more swiftly you will move towards your goals.

4

KNOW YOUR NUMBERS—THE KEY TO GROWTH AND FINANCIAL MASTERY

What gets measured gets managed.

—Peter Drucker

Newsflash: You're in the numbers game.

You would think that's obvious to a financial advisor. Yet, for so many, "knowing your numbers" often stops at knowing your clients' numbers inside and out. While that bit is crucial for you to be able to do a meticulous job for your clients, this chapter is about turning the spotlight onto *your* numbers. And not just the number of commissions you earn.

I invite you to start looking at your operations like an entrepreneur. Think expenses, profit, loss, net revenue, gross profit, and bonuses. Think of the number of hours that go into acquiring a client, warming them up, and then guiding them to a closed deal. After all those hours (and your hourly rate) are accounted for, was the sale profitable or a loss-making proposition for you? If you really want to do the thing right, then think about the hours that you will invest into servicing this client for years to come. Will you see them once a month or once a quarter for the tenure of their policy?

If adding all that up reveals a glaring red number indicating a long-term loss, it might be best to walk away from the deal, even if it is money in the bank today. It's a different way of thinking about the 'Lifetime Value' of a customer. Not just the financial value of a client for the duration of your relationship, but also the value of time and resources you will be investing in return for that monetary value.

When you start thinking about your numbers like an entrepreneur (because you are one!), how you perceive and utilise your time and resources will change, too.

When I talk about 'knowing your numbers,' I mean getting so specific about every facet of your financial advisory practice that nothing is left to chance. Whether it is your profit and loss statement, the return on investment (ROI) of your marketing campaigns, or the time spent per client interaction, each of these numbers holds valuable insight into the health and future of your business.

This chapter will explore why numbers are your most valuable asset in decision-making, how you can measure and manage growth, and why specificity is the difference that will allow you to jump from the struggle train to the exponential growth train.

WHY NUMBERS MATTER: OBJECTIVITY AND CLARITY

Clarity drives growth. Measuring and reading the right numbers creates the most objective clarity you can hope for. You get clear on what is and isn't working, where you're on target, and where you fall short. Feelings, assumptions, and anecdotal evidence can only take you so far; numbers provide the concrete data that lets you see, in real time, where you are and where you're heading.

Peter Drucker, one of the most celebrated management consultants and authors of the 20th century, famously explained that what gets measured gets managed.[8] This reasoning encapsulates the essence of this chapter. You set yourself up for intentional and strategic growth by consistently measuring and managing key financial metrics. Numbers remove ambiguity. They strip away emotions and allow you to make data-driven decisions that will push your business to the next level.

THE NUMBERS THAT MATTER MOST: A BREAKDOWN FOR FINANCIAL ADVISORS

If you want to grow your business, you need to know more than just how much money is coming in and going out. While those numbers are essential, they are just the tip of the iceberg. Let's break down the key metrics every financial advisor should be tracking.

1. REVENUE AND COMMISSIONS

This is the most obvious metric, but knowing your total earnings is not enough. You need to break it down by product, client type, and region (if applicable).

Where is most of your income coming from? What type of clients are generating the most revenue? What products are giving you the highest commissions? Knowing these answers allows you to double down on what's working and pivot away from what isn't. Remember that for sustained revenue growth, your proposition isn't something that simply earns you money; it's something that drives long-term value. Above all, your proposition—the problem you solve and the solution you offer—must be valuable to your client. This is the cornerstone of every great business or service: The client gains from working with you just as much, if not more, than you gain from working with them.

2. PROFIT AND LOSS (P&L)

Managing your profit and loss statement means going beyond just knowing your gross income and subtracting your expenses. A deeper dive into your P&L will reveal the cost of acquiring a client, your marketing expenditures, and how these numbers compare to your revenue. If your expenses are growing faster than your income, it's a sign you need to revisit your strategy, consider where you can cut costs, *or* work out if the increased expenses are setting you up for increased income. If that is the case, what does your return on investment look like, and how much time will you take to recover these returns?

3. CLIENT ACQUISITION COST (CAC)

How much are you spending to acquire a new client? This number includes your marketing budget, sales efforts, and any other resources used to bring in new business. Lowering your CAC can dramatically increase your profitability. You'll need to track each dollar spent on acquiring clients to understand if your methods are efficient or if there's room for improvement.

4. LIFETIME VALUE OF A CLIENT (LTV)

Knowing the lifetime value of each client is key to understanding how much you can spend on acquiring new ones. Let's say that your average check size today is $5,000. Essentially, selling one policy results in an average commission check of $5,000 for you. Then, you meet a client you know will generate $50,000 in total commissions over the next 15–20 years of working with you. So that one client's lifetime value is 10x your average commission check. Is that a profitable client for you? Does that lifetime value excite you? Does it make you believe you can serve this client even after you've spent the commission check(s)?

The Lifetime Value that makes sense for my business today is $2 million. That is to say, we expect to generate somewhere in the region of $2 million from a 25- to 30-year relationship with our clients by servicing their long-term life insurance and succession planning needs. That number has evolved and will probably continue to level up as our practice grows.

Take some time here to jot down what the Lifetime Value figure is relevant to you right now. This is not a one-size-fits-all number or a set-in-stone figure by any means! Make it yours, give it room to breathe, and evolve over time as your business model evolves.

If you follow my content or have stumbled upon my company, Successio Global, you know that the centre of our strategy is lifelong relationships. When I consider the lifetime value of a client, I generally think 20, 30, or 40 years ahead and all the possible ways we can serve them over the decades. This approach changes everything, from how we approach a client, qualify them as the right fit, and how we establish the relationship and build trust.

I have reviewed policies and advised clients for free for years, with my only goal being to establish a Know, Like, and Trust relationship. If and when they have a legacy planning need, I want it to be a no-brainer for them to think of me.

5. MARKETING ROI

Every dollar you spend on marketing should yield a return. Whether you're investing in digital ads, seminars, or personal branding efforts, track the effectiveness of your campaigns to ensure optimal results. What's working? What's not? Measuring your marketing ROI allows you to allocate resources effectively and discontinue initiatives that aren't producing a strong return.

Note: This could feel like a far-off goal for you. You may not be ready to launch a full-fledged marketing engine yet, which is ok. But I would like you to pause here and take a look at your current lead generation efforts. Chances are that you are doing some form of marketing and lead generation to put yourself in front of potential clients. Are you cold-calling? Are you paying for LinkedIn Sales Navigator to identify new clients? Are you attending networking events?

Each of these activities has a cost associated with it. Start tracking those costs. Also, if you have no personal brand or notable marketing efforts, then the best time to start was yesterday. The next best time to start is today.

6. TIME SPENT PER CLIENT

Time is your most valuable resource, and it's finite. You need to know how much time you spend on each client, from the first meeting to closing a deal. By measuring the time spent per client, you can identify inefficiencies and streamline your process. If certain clients are taking up a disproportionate amount of your time but aren't generating significant revenue, you'll need to rethink your approach to them.

The only way for you to determine if it is profitable to spend time on a case is to have determined your hourly rate.

If you haven't worked this out yet, I will give you a straightforward way to go about it. This formula might need a few tweaks that are specific to you and your business.

- **Step 1:** List out your commission checks from your top 10 clients (past or current). For example, a policy pulled in $10,000 in commissions for you.
- **Step 2:** For each policy sold, jot down the number of years you will be servicing this policy. Let's say 10 years.
- **Step 3:** Divide the total commission check by the number of years you will service this policy. $10,000 / 10 = $1,000. You now have a 'yearly' rate.
- **Step 4:** For every year, jot down the number of calls or meetings you will have with this client. Will you be investing a total of four hours per year? (A one-hour meeting every quarter?). That would be $1,000 / 4 = $250.

You now have an hourly rate. Doing this for all 10 clients will give you an 'average hourly rate.'

Let's assume your average hourly rate comes up to $200. Does it make sense to spend 20 hours on a client for a $2,000 commission check in that case? Not at all; that would be a loss-making proposition. Per this example, we assume you're operating as a solo operator. But what if you have a small admin or support team? If so, their 'hours' servicing this client also become a part of this calculation.

Get to work. Work out your hourly rate and start identifying your profitable versus non-profitable clients and cases. This might be uncomfortable, but it is the eye-opener you need to level up!

7. CONVERSION RATES

This metric applies to everything from prospecting to closing deals. How many of your initial leads turn into meetings? How many meetings turn into signed clients? How many signed deals lead to repeat business with existing clients? In 2024, for example, we'll be writing 60 per cent of our business from existing clientele. We've identified that on average, a whopping 79 per cent of our total annual revenue from 2021 to 2025 has come from repeat business in the form of policy upgrades, top-ups, and other opportunities to keep serving our client base.

Knowing your conversion rates at each stage of your sales funnel, including what happens after a sale, allows you to identify weak points and opportunities for improvement.

SPECIFICITY: THE SECRET TO EFFECTIVE MEASUREMENT

If there's one key takeaway from this chapter, it's that specificity is critical. Broad, vague numbers won't help you make informed decisions. You need to get granular with your data—down to every cent. Being specific allows you to pinpoint exactly what's working and what needs adjusting.

There's a reason why the most successful financial advisors obsess over details. Knowing your numbers to the smallest detail allows you to make those small, precise adjustments that lead to significant results over time. For example, it's time to rethink your approach if you're spending $2,500 on marketing each month and generating only $2,000 in commissions from those efforts. Targeting a different demographic or using a different platform may yield better results. However, if you don't track the exact ROI of your marketing efforts, you'll never know.

CASE STUDY: WHY SPECIFICITY WORKS

Consider the story of Jeff Bezos, the founder of Amazon. In the early days of Amazon, Bezos knew that the only way to scale effectively was to become obsessed with data. Every decision Amazon made was backed by detailed metrics. Bezos drilled down into every aspect of the company's operations—everything from shipping costs to the time it took to fulfil an order. By tracking every relevant metric, Amazon was able to innovate and make informed decisions that led to its dominance in the retail space.

While your financial advisory practice may not be on the scale of Amazon, the principle remains the same. Getting specific about your numbers allows you to optimise your business, improve client acquisition, and maximise your revenue.

HOW TO TRACK AND MANAGE YOUR NUMBERS: TOOLS AND SYSTEMS

The good news is that there are tools to help you track and manage your numbers effectively, so you don't need to do it all manually.

1. CLIENT RELATIONSHIP MANAGEMENT (CRM) TOOLS

A CRM system like Salesforce or HubSpot can help you track client data, including where each client is in the sales funnel, how much time you're spending on each one, and what your conversion rates are. Many CRMs also integrate with your marketing tools, allowing you to track the effectiveness of your campaigns.

2. EXPENSE TRACKING SOFTWARE

QuickBooks, FreshBooks, or Xero can help you track your expenses down to the last dollar. You can categorise spending, monitor your P&L, and generate reports to give you a clear view of where your money is going.

3. MARKETING ANALYTICS PLATFORMS

Tools like Google Analytics or social media tracking platforms (e.g., Hootsuite) can help you measure your marketing ROI. How much traffic are you getting from specific campaigns? How many leads are turning into prospects? The more data you have, the better you can optimise your marketing spend.

4. AUTOMATING FINANCIAL REPORTS

If manually calculating your P&L statement is overwhelming, consider automating your financial reports. Many accounting tools allow you to set up custom reports that are generated automatically, giving you real-time data without requiring manual effort.

COUNT YOUR WAY TO MDRT

For financial advisors aspiring to qualify for MDRT, numbers serve as a roadmap to guide your journey.

You need to know exactly where you are at all times—how many policies you've sold, how much commission you've generated, and how much you spend to acquire each client. This specificity allows you to make strategic adjustments to your business, doubling down on what's working and cutting out what's not.

Every successful advisor I know who has achieved MDRT qualification didn't get there by chance. They knew their numbers—intimately. They would be able to tell you, without hesitation, how many meetings they had each week, what their average commission per client was, and what their annual expense budget looked like. This level of precision is what separates the top performers from those who struggle to maintain consistent growth.

NUMBERS MASTERY PROCESS[IP]: ACTIONABLE STEPS TO START KNOWING YOUR NUMBERS

1. START WITH THE BASICS

If you're not tracking your revenue, expenses, and client acquisition costs down to the last detail, start there. You can't manage what you don't measure, so begin by getting a clear picture of your overall financial health. What are your monthly expenses? What are your top income-generating clients or products? How much are you spending on marketing? Understanding these foundational metrics will give you a baseline for improvement.

2. GET SPECIFIC WITH YOUR METRICS

Once you have the basics down, it's time to dig deeper. Get specific about each category of expense and income. Break down your revenue by product type, client segment, and region. Do the same for your expenses. For example, rather than simply listing "marketing expenses," break them down into categories like digital advertising, events, and referral programs. The more specific you get, the more clarity you will have.

3. TRACK YOUR MARKETING ROI

If you're spending money on marketing (and you should be), make sure you're tracking the return on investment for each campaign. This could mean monitoring the number of leads each campaign generates, the amount you spend per lead, and the percentage of those leads that convert into paying clients. By knowing your marketing numbers, you can determine what strategies are working and which ones aren't, allowing you to optimise your efforts and maximise your return.

4. USE TECHNOLOGY TO AUTOMATE

Leverage technology to track your numbers more efficiently. Tools like CRM systems, expense tracking software, and marketing analytics platforms can save you time and provide detailed insights. Automate as much of the data collection and reporting process as possible, allowing you to focus on interpreting the numbers rather than constantly gathering them.

5. REVIEW YOUR NUMBERS REGULARLY

Make it a habit to review your numbers regularly. This doesn't mean waiting until the end of the quarter or the fiscal year—make it a weekly or even a daily practice. Set aside time each week to review your financials, marketing metrics, and client acquisition costs. Regular check-ins will allow you to catch potential issues early and make adjustments before they become bigger problems.

6. SET BENCHMARKS AND GOALS

Use your numbers to set clear, measurable goals for your business. If you know your current client acquisition cost is $500 per client, set a goal to reduce that to $400. Alternatively, if your average commission per client is $2,000, aim to increase that by targeting higher-value clients. Numbers give you a clear picture of where you are and help you set realistic goals for where you want to be.

THE TL;DR VERSION

Numbers don't lie. They are the most objective source of feedback in your business, and they hold you accountable. Whether you're aiming for MDRT qualification, increasing commissions by 20 per cent this year, or simply looking to grow your client base, the numbers will tell you whether you're on track or need to make adjustments.

Think of numbers as your GPS. Just as your GPS navigator guides you to your destination by providing real-time data about your location, numbers show your business exactly where you stand with your goals. If you're off course, the numbers will tell you. They'll confirm that you're moving in the right direction or help you course-correct.

One of the greatest benefits of knowing your numbers is that they eliminate guesswork. Instead of relying on gut feelings or assumptions, you have concrete data to guide your decisions. You can look at your marketing spend and know with certainty whether it's producing a positive return. You can track your client acquisition costs and make informed decisions about where to allocate resources.

For financial advisors, numbers are particularly important because your business relies heavily on commissions. You need to know precisely how many clients you need to meet each month to hit your targets, how much you need to sell to reach MDRT qualification, and your revenue goals for the year. Without these numbers, you're flying blind.

5

TACTICS AND STRATEGY—THE BLUEPRINT FOR EXPONENTIAL GROWTH

It's not the will to win that matters—everyone has that.
It's the will to prepare to win that matters.

—Paul "Bear" Bryant

I n the world of financial advising, achieving exponential growth year after year and hitting big financial goals is not the result of random actions. If that were the case, we would see far more financial advisors climbing the ranks to MDRT and beyond. Instead, many advisors find themselves stuck at a certain income level for years or even decades despite working harder than ever.

The truth is, hard work alone is not enough. Some of the hardest-working advisors are often the ones who remain stagnant, pushing their limits without seeing corresponding growth. Why? Because growth—real, exponential growth—is not just about effort. It's about deploying the right tactics, guided by a solid strategy.

This chapter will delve into why tactical action backed by a solid strategy is essential to your success as a financial advisor, and how implementing this the right way can accelerate your journey to that big goal. We'll also explore research on tactical implementation and offer comparisons to high-level athletes, particularly Olympic champions, who exemplify the power of combining strategy and tactics to achieve extraordinary results.

WHY STRATEGY MATTERS MORE THAN HARD WORK

You've probably heard the saying, "Work smarter, not harder." A cliché, maybe, but it's been the cornerstone of my career for the last 12 years—the years in which I saw exponential growth.

Many advisors who remain stuck at the same income level year after year do so because they believe that working harder is the solution. They take more client meetings, work longer hours, and push themselves to the brink of burnout—only to find their income has barely budged.

The missing piece? Strategy.

Strategic Coach Co-Founder Dan Sullivan, whose ideas have been instrumental in shaping my own business, often talks about the difference between random activity or 'busy-ness' and intentional strategy. Without a clear strategy, even the hardest-working advisor is like a ship without a rudder, moving in no particular direction.

A solid strategy serves as your roadmap to success. It helps you clarify your goals, identify the most efficient path to reach them and determine the right tactics to deploy along the way. Importantly, a well-thought-out strategy ensures that every action you take is purposeful and aligned with your larger objectives, rather than a random act or bursts of productivity in the hopes of 'making it.'

For example, when I hit my first $100,000 commission year, I had a strategy that focused on serving clients who needed larger policies. I wasn't just taking on more clients. I was specifically targeting those who would move the needle.

My strategy evolved as I grew from $100,000 to $500,000 and eventually hit the million-dollar commission mark, but it was never random. Every tactic I used and every client I pursued was part of a bigger plan.

When I first got into the life insurance business back in 1999, the goal was simple: I wanted to create a little 'pocket money' for myself

(I lived at home with my parents, so I didn't have 'living expenses' or bills to pay), and my more egoistic goal was to prove my dad wrong—to show him that I could absolutely make it and stand on my own two feet.

Over time, well, I grew up. I had bigger aspirations, grounded more in my goals for me rather than to show anyone what I was capable of, and I started 'adulting.' I moved out, met my wife, and started a family. With every passing year, my financial needs and lifestyle expenses grew, and my income goals grew, too.

Today, my goals are more impact-oriented. In my Life Insurance practice, it has taken us 25 years to hit '$1 Billion in Cover We Are Responsible For'. My goal is to reach the $3 billion mark in the next five years. With Successio Academy, my goal is to serve five million financial advisors with our programs over the next five years and give them the tools and support necessary to achieve their career goals.

Are there financial wins for me attached to these goals? Of course! However, that's no longer the driving force for me. The driver behind my goals today is the desire to make an impact.

THE ROLE OF TACTICS: THE 'HOW' OF ACHIEVING YOUR GOALS

If strategy is the 'what' and 'why' behind your actions, tactics are the 'how.' Tactics are the specific actions you take to implement your strategy. This could mean everything from how you structure your client meetings, how you market your services, and how you follow up with prospects.

The key to success lies in consistently executing the right tactics. But here's the thing: Not every tactic will work for you. You need to experiment, adjust, and refine your approach to discover what works best for your unique practice and goals.

Think of tactics like the training regimen of an Olympic athlete. An Olympic sprinter doesn't just 'run more' or 'run harder' to win a gold medal. There's a specific strategy behind their training that dictates how they should train, what exercises they need to focus on, and how to optimise their nutrition and recovery. The tactics they employ in the gym, on the track, and in their mental conditioning are carefully crafted to align with their overall strategy.

The same is true for financial advisors. Some of the best advisors I've met at MDRT don't just work harder; they work smarter by deploying tactics that move them closer to their goals. They experiment with different marketing strategies, test client engagement techniques, and adopt tools that help them manage their time and resources more efficiently.

THE POWER OF TACTICAL IMPLEMENTATION

Research shows that tactical implementation is one of the most critical factors in achieving long-term success.[9] In the book *The Four Disciplines of Execution*, Chris McChesney highlights that organisations and individuals often fail to reach their goals because they focus too much on strategy and not enough on tactical execution.[10] He argues that while strategy provides direction, it's the consistent, focused execution of tactics that ultimately drives results.

What does this mean for you? It means that the big ideas, the motivation, and even the strategic clarity you experience after you've read a book (this book, for instance) or heard a top-performing advisor speak will not carry you to the finish line.

Your results are on the other side of focused action. You will need to implement the right tactics day in and day out to see progress. This could mean committing to a certain number of client meetings each week, sending a specific number of follow-up emails, or ensuring you're staying on top of your prospect pipeline.

Tactics, however, are not just about execution—they also include the tools and systems you use to operate more efficiently. For example, Dan Sullivan's Entrepreneurial Time System® is a tactical approach to time management that has been a game-changer in my own practice. By breaking time into three distinct categories—Free, Focus, Buffer Days®—you ensure that your time is spent in a way that maximises productivity and prevents burnout. This system allowed me to focus on high-value activities, like client meetings and business development, while giving me the downtime I needed to recharge.

TESTING TACTICS AND FINDING WHAT WORKS FOR YOU

One of the most important lessons I've learned in my career is that not every tactic will work for every advisor. The strategies and tactics that helped me hit my first $100,000 in commissions were not the same ones that got me to $500,000, and they certainly weren't the ones that helped me cross the million-dollar mark.

The key is to test different tactics, keep track of the results, and refine your approach based on what works. Early in my career, I picked up various tactics from MDRT programs, audio and video tapes, books, and conversations with my peers. I would put these ideas to the test, and the ones that worked became part of my long-term strategy for that specific goal. The ones that didn't? I discarded them without hesitation and moved on to try the next method.

There's a famous quote attributed to Thomas Edison during his attempts to invent the modern electric light bulb. A reporter reportedly questioned him on his 10,000 failed attempts, to which Edison replied: "I have not failed 10,000 times. I have not failed once. I have succeeded in proving that those 10,000 ways will not work."

Spoken like a true champion, wouldn't you say? This 'never give up' approach is what ultimately, inevitably leads to success. This is why it's so important to stay adaptable. Not every tactic is going to work for you, and that's okay. The point is to experiment, measure the results, and determine your success formula. Eventually, you will land on the strategy that works best for you.

REAL-WORLD TACTICS: MY OWN JOURNEY

Let me give you a glimpse into some of the tactics that have worked for me as I've grown my business. A few years into my career, I realised that one of the most effective ways to increase my income was to focus on the 'Right-Fit Client,' a concept I learned from Strategic Coach. The idea is simple: not every client is a good fit for your business. I was asked a question in one of my Strategic Coach workshops that has become the cornerstone for the way we build our client base today: "Who do you want to be a hero to?"

Focusing on clients who align with your values and goals can build more productive, long-term relationships, which often result in higher commissions. Even if you offer free advice to them, and you know they're not gearing up for a transaction anytime soon, just knowing that you're serving a potential right-fit client with that advice will benefit you in the long run. If you're giving up your time and energy for free, you might as well do it for the person you want to be a hero to!

As I grew my practice, I started to adopt more specific tactics for time management, marketing, and client engagement. One tactic that helped me immensely was setting aside specific 'Focus Days' for client meetings and business development, and 'Buffer Days' for catching up on administrative work. This simple time-management tactic allowed me to maximise my energy on the days when I needed to perform at my best while ensuring that I didn't burn out.

Another tactic that proved incredibly valuable was my approach to marketing. Early on, I realised that not all marketing channels were created equal. Instead of spreading myself thin across multiple platforms, I tested different marketing tactics and focused on the ones that yielded the best results. This allowed me to streamline my marketing efforts and focus my resources on what was working, rather than wasting time and money on tactics that weren't delivering results.

I also decided to go all in on personal branding. At this point, Successio Global, my company, didn't exist, and personal branding was the marketing strategy that allowed me to create the deepest Know, Like, and Trust factor with potential clients.

I hired an expert to help me implement the strategy and identify the best tactics. Some of our tactics included (and still do to this day) creating long-form content and articles, developing case studies in both video and article formats, sharing personal anecdotes and stories from my life beyond work, and firing up my speaking career. You can find all my content by scanning this QR code.

YOU WILL GET SOME OF THIS WRONG—AND THAT'S OKAY

Not every tactic you try will work. Some will fail miserably, and that's perfectly okay. In fact, it's part of the process. Testing tactics, refining your approach, and learning from failure are crucial steps toward success.

When I look back on my twenty-five years in this industry, I can point to numerous tactics that didn't work out as I had hoped. I've tried marketing campaigns that fell flat, client engagement strategies that didn't resonate, and sales pitches that got the door (or phone) slammed in my face. My mentor in my early days encouraged me to go out there and test even the cheesiest of pitches to see if they would work—just to 'collect' my 'No's because they would be the stepping stones that allowed me to get closer to the strategies that work.

This process of trial and error is not just inevitable; it's necessary. If you're unwilling to test new ideas, you'll struggle to discover the tactics that will unlock your practice's next level of growth. The key is to be strategic about your testing. Implement new tactics one at a time, measure the results, and iterate based on what you learn. Over time, you'll develop a toolkit of proven tactics that will drive your success.

EXECUTION ENGINE[IP]: ACTIONABLE STEPS FOR IMPLEMENTING TACTICS AND STRATEGY IN YOUR PRACTICE

Here are a few steps to get you started on building a solid strategy and deploying the right tactics in your financial advisory practice.

1. CLARIFY YOUR STRATEGY

Start by defining your long-term goals. Whether qualifying for MDRT, increasing your revenue by 50 per cent, or building a client base with more of your right-fit clients, your strategy should revolve around these goals. Once your strategy is clear, you can start identifying the tactics that will help you achieve it.

2. TEST AND TRACK YOUR TACTICS

When implementing new tactics, be methodical in your approach. Try one new tactic at a time, and track your results closely. Whether it's a new marketing approach, a change in how you structure client meetings or a time-management system, measure the impact on your business. Keep the tactics that work and discard the ones that don't. Don't be afraid to make quick changes and keep your approach flexible.

3. ADAPT AND EVOLVE

As your business grows, so too should your strategy and tactics. What works to get you to $100,000 in commissions may not be the same tactics that get you to the half-a-million mark. Be prepared to adapt and evolve your approach over time. The best financial advisors are those who remain open to change and continually refine their strategies to meet evolving needs.

4. LEARN FROM PEERS AND MENTORS

Don't reinvent the wheel. There's tremendous value in learning from those who have already walked your path. Engage with peers and mentors to pick up proven tactics and strategies. Learning from others' successes and failures will save time and effort.

5. FOCUS ON THE RIGHT-FIT CLIENTS

One of my most valuable tactics is focusing on the right clients. Not every client will be a good fit for your business. In fact, some will be a toxic drain on your energy and resources. Apply choice. Choice is *not* a luxury that you unlock when you hit a certain level of success.

Identify your ideal client who aligns with your values and financial goals and focus your efforts on serving them. This approach boosts your income and helps you build a more sustainable, fulfilling practice.

THE COMPOUND EFFECT OF STRATEGY AND TACTICS

In *The Compound Effect*, Darren Hardy explains how small, smart choices, when repeated consistently over time, lead to massive success.[11] This concept applies perfectly to the deployment of tactics in a financial advisory practice. The tactics you choose to implement may seem small or insignificant at first—a tweak to your client meeting structure here, a new follow-up process there—but when executed consistently, these small changes compound into exponential growth.

The financial advisors who consistently achieve MDRT status year after year and eventually hit Court of the Table and Top of the Table status are not doing so because of one big move or tactic. They succeed because they consistently execute a strategy built on a foundation of proven tactics. Over time, the cumulative effect of their efforts leads to extraordinary results.

THE TL;DR VERSION

To achieve exponential growth in your career as a financial advisor, you need both a solid strategy and the right tactics. One without the other will leave you stuck in place. A brilliant strategy is useless if you don't implement the right tactics to bring it to life. Likewise, deploying random tactics without a clear strategy is like running on a treadmill—you expend energy but don't move forward.

By clarifying your strategy, testing and refining your tactics, and learning from successes and failures, you'll unlock the next level of growth in your business. Whether you're aiming for MDRT qualification, your first $500,000 year, or working towards a single check that qualifies you for Top of the Table, the combination of strategic thinking and tactical execution will get you there.

Not every tactic will work, and that's okay. The key is to keep experimenting, refining, and moving forward. As long as you stay committed to your strategy and open to testing new ideas, you'll find the tactics that work for you—and your success will be anything but random.

6

RIGHT-FIT CLIENTS

*Both of those clients could earn you the same commission
check but cost you in very different ways.*

—Rickson D'Souza

I cannot begin to tell you how true that quote has rung throughout my career. There is always more than one way to earn a paycheck. Each of those ways will present different challenges. But some of those challenges will help you to grow, while others will, in the course of time, prove to be less growth, more drain.

When I was a young, impressionable advisor hungry for ways to grow in the industry, I formed an idea based on something I saw at MDRT. Many of the more successful, seemingly experienced advisors had two badges pinned to their chests: a shiny Top of the Table badge and, right under, they had another badge that said '150 Lives.' These advisors had insured 150 lives in the past year. I automatically connected the two as cause and effect. I decided that the way to the Top of the Table was by finding and selling policies to 150 clients.

That year, in 2008, I left MDRT with two goals: To earn the 150 Lives badge and, consequently, the Top of the Table badge.

In 2009, I returned to MDRT with my gleaming Top of the Table badge. But I had only hit '132 Lives' and had one less shiny badge that I wasn't flashing around—total and complete burnout.

Over the next couple of years, I continued to achieve the Top of the Table goal, averaging 130-140 cases per year, but I never quite reached that 150 mark. And then came the big shift in my business.

During that period, I joined Strategic Coach and was introduced to the concepts of the 'Right-Fit Client' and the 'Minimum Check Size' that we were gunning for. Those two concepts changed everything about my business. We went from working with approximately 140 clients a year to taking on only seven new clients a year. Our average check size per case went up from $12,000 to $40,000. The rest of our commission for that year came from repeat business with existing clients and cases.

It took us years of fine-tuning, refining, and working with various clients to narrow down and arrive at a laser-sharp client description.

Here is what I know to be true: My starting point wasn't so different from a lot of financial advisors' early days in practice. For many financial advisors, the idea of attracting more clients is often synonymous with success. Most financial services companies and insurance companies also deal with the masses. As a result, they need advisors to engage with the masses, and 'more contracts signed' is a straightforward goal to aim for.

But what if I told you that the key to long-term growth and fulfilment in your career isn't about chasing more clients but finding the right ones?

Before I started focusing on my Right-Fit Clients, I was chasing commission checks, constantly trying to sign more clients to grow my income. We trained our team of sixty advisors to 'do more business,' too. However, over time, I began to realise that this could hardly be the only way to succeed.

For one, the harder I worked, the more I realised that not all clients are created equal. In fact, some clients can actually drain your energy and resources, taking up hours of your time and coming up with one problem after another, while others elevate your business and help you grow exponentially. This is the Profitability Paradox^{IP}. Both of those clients could earn you the same commission check, but cost you in very different ways.

How do you identify those clients? More importantly, how do you find more clients like them?

That is exactly what I will break down for you in this chapter. Over the next few pages, I'll introduce you to the concept of Right-Fit Clients, the importance of discovering who they are for your unique practice, and the steps you need to take to identify and attract them.

HOW I DISCOVERED MY RIGHT-FIT CLIENTS

My own journey to finding my Right-Fit Client was born out of necessity. As I previously mentioned, I found myself in over $550,000 worth of debt, which quickly ballooned to $2 million after exiting two businesses on the same day. As with any sum like that looming over you, it was debt that I wanted to clear as quickly as possible. I knew that small commission checks wouldn't cut it, so I began to aim for larger deals and higher commission checks. This led me to the HNW and UHNW client space, which, after years of study and experience, became my speciality.

While Strategic Coach introduced me to this game-changing Right-Fit Client strategy, I have utilised other tools from Strategic Coach, as well as my own insights and experiments, to further refine my right-fit client profile. Based on this, I have created a Right-Fit Client guide, which you can download by scanning the QR code below. This guide will help you identify your Right-Fit Client.

At the start of this process, I'll be honest and say that it was, in fact, about the money. Working with larger clients meant larger commissions, something I needed to manage my financial challenges at the time. But over time, as I refined my approach, I realised something even more valuable: these clients shared my values. They understood the value of what I offered and, more importantly, they respected it. I felt at ease around this clientele because I shared their entrepreneurial mindset and philosophy on success, family, relationships, and other areas of life. Further, the more specialised I became at solving their succession problems and serving their life insurance needs, the more at ease they felt with me. I 'spoke their language,' so to speak.

As of the writing of this book in 2025, my team and I work with only four new clients each year, and in 2023 alone, we generated twelve times the Top of the Table numbers with those four clients. And a quick update is that we closed 2025 at almost double the 2023 earnings. The clients we take on fit a very stringent set of criteria that we have developed—they check all the boxes on our Right-Fit Client list.

It wasn't always like this, I assure you. It took years to refine my understanding of who my Right-Fit Clients were, and even more time to build a network of introducers and clients who consistently refer me to people that fit my criteria. But I can tell you this: working with the right clients—those who share your values, respect your expertise, and align with your goals—makes all the difference.

Remember, your Right-Fit Client may not be a high-net-worth (HNW) or ultra-high-net-worth (UHNW) individual. You might choose to or need to work with more than four clients a year to meet your goals. The point isn't to follow my exact path but to discover your ideal clients.

Now, let's talk about how you can discover your Right-Fit Clients.

STEPS TO DISCOVERING YOUR RIGHT-FIT CLIENT

The process of discovering your Right-Fit Clients isn't something that happens overnight. It requires thoughtful reflection, analysis, and trial and error. But once you clearly understand who these clients are, your business will start to evolve in ways you never imagined.

Below is the Client Fit Evaluation Framework[IP]: the steps to follow to help you define your ideal Right-Fit Client.

1. SET CLEAR GOALS

The first step in identifying your Right-Fit Clients is setting clear, specific business goals. As outlined in the workbook, clarity is key. If your goal is to grow your income, don't just say, "I want to make more money." Be specific. For example, you could aim for "$500,000 in commissions by the end of the year." This specificity will help guide your search for the types of clients who can help you reach that goal.

Remember: This is a two-way street. If your clients are helping you hit your goals, it is only because you are helping them hit theirs. You're looking for the best blend of 'most profitable' and 'most profiting' clients. They're winning as a result of your product, service, and solutions. And that leads perfectly into the next step.

2. IDENTIFY YOUR BEST CLIENTS

Review your current client base and identify your top 10 most valuable clients. These are the clients you enjoy working with, who respect your expertise, and who energise you. As you analyse this list, you'll start to see patterns. Do these clients share certain characteristics? Are they in similar industries? Do they have common personality traits? Understanding what makes these clients your best clients will help you identify similar prospects.

3. ANALYSE THE TRAITS OF YOUR BEST CLIENTS

Once you've identified your top 10 best clients, take some time to analyse what makes them great to work with. Is it their communication style? Their financial standing? The mutual respect in the relationship? The ability to take your advice seriously and act on it? This step is critical because it helps you define the key qualities you should look for in future clients.

4. LIST YOUR WORST CLIENTS

Just as important as knowing who your best clients are is knowing who your worst clients are. Take some time to list your 10 worst clients. These are the people who drain your energy, make unreasonable demands, or constantly question your advice. Understanding what makes these clients difficult to work with is just as important as knowing what makes your best clients great. This will help you avoid taking on clients who don't align with your values and goals.

5. COMPARE THE COMMON QUALITIES OF BOTH LISTS

Now that you have both lists—your best and worst clients— it's time to compare them. What traits do your best clients share? What traits do your worst clients have in common? This exercise will give you a clear picture of who you should target and who you should avoid. The more specific you can get, the better. For example, if you notice that your worst clients tend to be highly demanding but unwilling to act on your advice, you'll know to steer clear of clients who exhibit those traits.

6. CALCULATE HOW MANY RIGHT-FIT CLIENTS YOU NEED

Once you've identified the traits of your Right-Fit Clients, it's time to figure out how many of these clients you need to meet your income goals. Divide your income goal by your average ticket size. That will give you the number of clients you need per year.

> No. of Clients Required =
> Total Annual Income Goal / Average Ticket Size

For instance, if your goal is $200,000 and your average ticket size is $20,000, you know you need 10 clients to hit your goal. This number will help you focus your efforts and avoid taking on too many clients who aren't a good fit.

7. LEVERAGE INTRODUCERS AND REFERRALS

Your current best clients are your greatest asset when it comes to finding more Right-Fit Clients. Think of three to five clients from your best list who would likely introduce you to others like them. These introductions are incredibly valuable because they come with built-in trust and credibility. Referrals from Right-Fit Clients tend to result in more Right-Fit Clients, creating a positive cycle of growth for your business.

HOW TO FIND YOUR RIGHT-FIT CLIENTS

Finding your Right-Fit Clients isn't about casting the widest net but fishing in the right pond. Not all of these approaches will work for every client niche, and not all of them will be right for you as an individual. Pick the ideas that resonate most and seem like a good fit for your Right-Fit Client.

Here are some effective ways to help find your Right-Fit Clients. These are strategies that have worked well for me.

1. BUILD YOUR PERSONAL BRAND AND DIGITAL PRESENCE

If you want to attract Right-Fit Clients, you need to be where they're looking. Build a strong personal brand that speaks directly to their needs and values. Use social media, your website, and content marketing to position yourself as the go-to expert in your niche. Consistency in your messaging will naturally filter out clients who aren't a good fit and draw in those who are.

2. THE "NATURALLY OCCURRING PERSON" STRATEGY

Want to build trust with Right-Fit Clients? Start by showing up where they are, not as an outsider but as part of their world. Whether it's joining the same golf club, attending the same charity events, or becoming part of the social circles they frequent, being a "naturally occurring person" in their environment makes the connection feel authentic.

It's less about networking and more about feeling a sense of belonging. Scan this QR code to watch a short training video called "7 Unlikely Places to Look for Prospects."

3. INTRODUCTIONS FROM CURRENT RIGHT-FIT CLIENTS

Your best clients often know others like them. Don't be afraid to ask for introductions from clients you already consider Right-Fit. You could go the 'asking for a referral' route, but that leaves too much to chance. So consider a more mindful relationship-nurturing approach to stay top-of-mind for your introducers. They already know and trust you – deepen that relationship to make it easy for them to send relevant, high-quality leads and opportunities your way.

4. GET INVOLVED IN NICHE COMMUNITIES

Align yourself with the organisations, online forums, or professional associations that serve your Right-Fit Clients.

This is where you'll find prospects who are looking for someone with your expertise.

This is by no means an exhaustive list. Once you have even a rough idea of your Right-Fit Client profile, you can brainstorm all the various ways in which you can 'intersect paths' with these individuals. Are they a specific type of professional? Do they have interests or hobbies that tell you where they might spend their evenings or weekends? Are they tech enthusiasts who are likely to be following content put out by an influencer you follow, too?

All of these details can open up ways and opportunities to think about how you can use what you know to show up and start building relationships with these individuals. Remember, you are not showing up in these common spaces to 'pitch' to them. You are showing up to connect with them and open the door for potential collaboration in the near (or distant) future.

For this prospecting exercise, please apply the same principles we have discussed so far: set a goal, constantly measure your metrics, and adjust your strategy to achieve the best outcomes and results.

This is one of the most expansive trainings within The Advisor's Growth Program. To learn more about the program, scan this QR code to indicate your interest and join the waitlist. We'll share details about upcoming intakes and other relevant information.

THE POWER OF RIGHT-FIT CLIENTS

Identifying and working with Right-Fit Clients is one of the most important steps you can take to grow your financial advisory practice. It's not about working harder or taking on more clients—it's about working smarter and focusing on the clients who align with your values, respect your expertise, and help you achieve your goals.

By following the steps outlined in this chapter, you'll discover who your Right-Fit Clients are and create a roadmap for attracting and working with more of them. This, in turn, will lead to greater satisfaction, higher commissions, and a more sustainable, fulfilling career.

The journey to finding your Right-Fit Clients may take time, but once you've identified them, your practice will transform in ways you never thought possible.

THE TL;DR VERSION

Success doesn't necessarily come from serving more clients. It comes from serving the right ones.

In the early years of my career, as a newbie at MDRT, I believed that insuring 150 lives a year was the golden path to Top of the Table success. And while I came close to that target and even reached the Top of the Table, the result wasn't just a professional achievement, but also personal burnout.

Everything changed when I shifted from volume to value. Through Dan Sullivan's Strategic Coach, I discovered the concept of the Right-Fit Client, clients who are aligned with your values, respect your expertise, and make doing business energising rather than exhausting.

With a refined focus, I transitioned from onboarding 130+ clients a year to taking on just seven new clients, yet still exceeded the Top of the Table threshold. Today, we take on four new clients a year and achieve milestones like 12 times Top of the Table in a given year.

This chapter walks you through how to identify your Right-Fit Clients using a 7-step process:

1. Set Clear Goals
2. Identify Your Best Clients
3. Analyse Their Traits
4. List Your Worst Clients
5. Compare Both Lists
6. Calculate How Many Right-Fit Clients You Need
7. Leverage Referrals & Introducers

I also share practical strategies to attract Right-Fit Clients—from building your personal brand to becoming a "naturally occurring person" in their world.

The bottom line: Your energy, income, and fulfilment skyrocket when you work with people who truly fit. Don't chase everyone. Serve the few who matter most.

7

OBSESSION—FUELING YOUR SUCCESS

You must be obsessed. You must be. You have to be consumed by what you do. If you are not, you will fail. Success is not something you can casually pursue.

—Grant Cardone, *Be Obsessed or Be Average*

Be Obsessed or Be Average is one of the first audiobooks I ever listened to. That audiobook—the message, Grant's delivery of it, the conviction in his voice—got me through some of the most gruelling training sessions I did as I prepped to run my first ultra-marathon, Marathon Des Sables, as a beginner runner with little prior running experience.

If one thing separates the ultra-successful from everyone else, it's obsession—the drive to pursue your goals relentlessly, day in and day out, without distraction or dilution. Obsession is the fuel that propels you forward when things get tough. The fire keeps you going when others have long since quit. If you want to achieve real, lasting success—hitting your first six-figure commission year, qualifying for MDRT, or completing another impossible goal in another area of your life—get obsessed.

I know this idea might have you thinking: That can't be healthy... An 'obsession' with anything can't be healthy! But that view is a misinterpretation of what it truly means to be obsessed with a goal.

In this chapter, we'll explore why obsession is vital for success, and address the common objections to obsession, particularly the idea that it leads to imbalance.

WHAT DOES IT MEAN TO BE OBSESSED?

Obsession, in the context of success, is about single-minded focus. It's about waking up every day with your goal front and centre in your mind. It's about putting your energy, your time, and your resources into achieving that goal, because you believe in it so deeply that anything less than total commitment feels inadequate.

Grant Cardone describes obsession as the "rocket fuel" for achieving massive success.[12] He argues that you can't afford to be merely interested in your goals—you have to be obsessed. In his book, he explains that obsession isn't about working yourself to exhaustion for the sake of it. Rather, it's about aligning everything in your life toward a single, powerful objective.

When you're obsessed, you're driven. You're consumed by the need to reach your target, and this doesn't feel like a burden; it feels like purpose. Obsession gives you a sense of urgency that pushes you to make things happen faster, be more creative, and stay resilient in the face of setbacks. Without this level of passion and commitment, goals become dreams—nice ideas that never materialise.

For me, obsession was what drove me through the most challenging years of my career. When I was in debt, trying to claw my way out, I wasn't just working hard, 'trying' to get rid of it. I was obsessed with clearing that debt and eventually scaling to a seven-figure business. That obsession shaped every decision I made, from the clients I pursued to the strategies I implemented. It wasn't a burden—it was my driving force.

WHY OBSESSION IS CRUCIAL FOR FINANCIAL ADVISORS

In the world of financial advising, obsession is often the difference between incremental growth and exponential success. Why? Because financial advisors operate in a highly competitive industry. Your clients have choices, and your products are often similar to those of your competitors. Standing out requires more than just showing up—it requires a relentless pursuit of excellence, which happens to be a side effect of obsession.

When you're obsessed with your goals, it shows in everything you do. Your clients can feel it. They sense your commitment, your determination, and your passion for helping them succeed. This energy is contagious. It's what turns prospects into long-term clients and builds a referral network of people who trust you implicitly.

Obsession also drives you to continually refine your approach. It forces you to study your industry, learn from your competitors, and innovate. When you're obsessed, you don't settle for 'good enough.' You're always looking for ways to improve, to deliver more value, and to push the boundaries of what's possible. This mindset is what separates average advisors from the top performers—the ones who achieve MDRT, Court of the Table, Top of the Table, 10x TOT, and beyond.

THE COMMON OBJECTION: 'ISN'T OBSESSION UNHEALTHY?'

One of the most common objections to the idea of obsession is that it creates imbalance. People worry that being overly focused on a goal will consume their lives, lead to burnout, and strain their personal relationships. They imagine obsession as an all-consuming force that leaves no room for anything else.

There is some truth to the concern that obsession, if left unchecked, can lead to burnout. But this happens when obsession is misunderstood or mismanaged. Obsession doesn't mean ignoring every other aspect of your life—it means aligning everything in your life to support your goal.

For example, when you're obsessed with building your financial advisory business, you might spend long hours working on your strategy, meeting with clients, and refining your tactics. But if you're truly obsessed with success, you'll also recognise the importance of health, relationships, and personal fulfilment in achieving that success.

Obsession doesn't require you to sacrifice everything else; it requires you to make everything else work in service of your goal.

THE HEALTHY WAY TO BE OBSESSED: A COUNTERARGUMENT

Let's address the counterargument: Obsession, when done right, is not unhealthy—it's the opposite. It provides clarity, focus, and a sense of purpose that many people lack. In his book, Cardone argues that obsession actually helps you create balance, because it forces you to prioritise the things that matter most.[13]

Here's how obsession can create balance rather than destroy it.

1. OBSESSION CREATES STRUCTURE

When you're obsessed with your goal, you become incredibly disciplined. You start structuring your days in a way that supports your goal. This structure often leads to more time for other important areas of your life because you no longer waste time on distractions or unimportant activities. For instance, my training runs for the Marathon des Sables were scheduled between 11 a.m. and 3 p.m., on both weekends *and* weekdays. This simulated the heat, the burning sun – in short, the desert running conditions I would be dealing with during the race. As opposed to 'throwing me off', this mandatory training block allowed me to become more efficient with my working hours. My 8 a.m. to 11 a.m. block and my 3 p.m. to 5 p.m. blocks were 'super-focus' blocks for me.

2. OBSESSION FUELS HEALTH AND WELL-BEING

Being obsessed with your goal often leads you to take better care of your health and well-being. Why? Because you realise that achieving your goal requires mental and physical peak performance. Just like an Olympic athlete wouldn't skip their training or nutrition plan, someone obsessed with success in business knows that health is a critical component of high performance.

3. OBSESSION STRENGTHENS RELATIONSHIPS

When you're clear about your goals and what you're working toward, you become more intentional about the relationships you nurture. You'll start surrounding yourself with people who support your obsession and distance yourself from those who drain your energy. Obsession sharpens your focus on who is important in your life and who aligns with your vision.

4. OBSESSION PROVIDES FULFILMENT

Finally, obsession isn't about deprivation—it's about fulfilment. When you're obsessed with achieving a goal, every step forward feels meaningful. You're driven by a sense of purpose, and this creates a deep sense of satisfaction. Working toward your goal can become just as fulfilling as achieving it.

People who believe that obsession is unhealthy often haven't experienced the true power of aligning their lives with a compelling goal. They see obsession as exhausting or overwhelming, but in reality, obsession creates clarity and simplifies decision-making. You're no longer distracted by shiny objects or trivial pursuits when you're obsessed. You know what you want and are willing to do what it takes to get there.

The key here is the Focused Effort Principle[IP]: It's not 'Do whatever it takes.' It's 'Do what it takes.' The secret is to check in on all the areas of your life that are important to you, including your values and ethics, and ensure that your obsession to excel, serve, and grow in all of these areas is being met.

THE DIFFERENCE BETWEEN OBSESSION AND BURNOUT

Burnout occurs when you work hard on something that doesn't align with your true passions or values. It happens when you're grinding away without a clear purpose, constantly feeling like you're falling short of your goals.

Obsession, on the other hand, is invigorating. When you're obsessed with your goal, the work itself becomes enjoyable because you know it's moving you closer to what you want. Even when you're working long hours or facing challenges, you feel energised by your progress.

I've experienced both. My burnout came when I was on track with what I call 'misdirected ambition.' I felt burnt out in my two wrong-fit business partnerships and spent hours 'managing' the relationship dynamic with my business partners.

I felt burnt out when heading a team of sixty advisors and managing all the business administration aspects of the practice, rather than doing what I am best at: Finding, nurturing the relationship with, and servicing a specifically defined right-fit client.

When I was pouring all my energy into those misaligned goals and activities, it led to burnout. But today, even if I stay up at night sorting out a problem for a client, even if I take those 8 p.m. calls with my business collaborators in the U.S. on high-impact projects, it never feels like burnout. Today, it's a healthy, vision-aligned, impact-driven action.

HEALTHY OBSESSION FRAMEWORK[IP]: ACTIONABLE STEPS TO FOSTER BALANCED PURSUIT OF EXCELLENCE

1. DEFINE YOUR VISION CLEARLY

What is the one goal that you're willing to be obsessed with? Write it down. Be specific. Whether it's achieving MDRT status, building a seven-figure practice, or becoming the go-to advisor for a particular niche, clarity is key. Without a clear target, you can't direct your obsession effectively.

2. ALIGN YOUR ENVIRONMENT

Make sure your professional and personal environment supports your obsession. This means setting boundaries, removing distractions, and surrounding yourself with people who believe in your vision and are willing to help you achieve it. Create a space that nurtures your drive, not one that pulls you away from it.

3. EMBRACE THE PROCESS

Obsession is a journey, not a destination. There will be ups and downs, wins and losses. What matters is that you stay the course and commit to the process. Every setback is an opportunity to refine your approach and get closer to your goal. Obsession gives you the resilience to push through challenges and keep moving forward.

4. AVOID BURNOUT BY RECOGNISING THE LONG GAME

Obsession doesn't mean sprinting until you collapse. It means playing the long game, pacing yourself, and making sure that your energy is sustainable. Recognise when you need to recharge and allow yourself the time to rest, so you can return stronger. Obsession is about consistency, not over-exertion.

5. MEASURE YOUR PROGRESS

To stay obsessed, you need to see progress. This is why tracking your results, celebrating milestones, and adjusting your tactics is crucial. When you see how far you've come, it fuels your obsession to keep going. Whether closing a major deal, hitting a new income milestone, or landing a Right-Fit Client, acknowledge your wins.

THE TL;DR VERSION

Obsession is a non-negotiable ingredient for extraordinary success. If you're not all-in and consumed by the drive to achieve your goals, you're settling for mediocrity. And mediocrity, in a world as competitive as financial advising, means stagnation.

But here's the thing: Obsession doesn't have to look the same for everyone. For me, my obsession began with clearing debt. Still, it evolved into something much bigger—a relentless pursuit of working with the best clients, building a high-value business, and ultimately finding financial freedom. What I learned along the way is that obsession is deeply personal. It's not about copying someone else's path or adopting someone else's goal. It's about finding what drives you and putting everything behind that.

You might be obsessed with achieving MDRT status or striving to build a thriving practice that caters to a specific niche. Whatever your goal, the obsession has to come from within. It has to light you up and make you willing to go the extra mile, even when things get tough. It becomes crucial here for these goals to be yours, not some arbitrary goal set by someone else. It's hard to become obsessed with someone else's goal.

Ultimately, obsession is the key to achieving anything worth having in life. The goals you're chasing, whether they are financial, personal, or professional, won't happen by accident. They require your full commitment, your relentless drive, and, yes, your obsession. Don't shy away from it. Lean into it, harness it, and use it to propel you toward your vision. When you make your goal the centre of everything you do, you'll find that success isn't just possible, it's inevitable.

This one quality, my ability to become obsessed with my goals, has helped me stay on the path and achieve what most others deemed 'impossible' in many areas of my life: fitness, family, friendships, business . . . you name it.

8

LIFE—ACHIEVING TRUE FULFILMENT BEYOND FINANCIAL SUCCESS

Balance is not something you find; it is something you create.

—Jana Kingsford

You've worked hard, set ambitious goals, and pursued success relentlessly. You've likely heard the phrase "success comes at a price," but what if that price is too high?

In pursuing financial achievement, it's easy to lose sight of the things that truly matter most: your family, loved ones, health, and overall well-being. The truth is, all the financial success in the world means very little if it comes at the cost of the life you want to live.

This chapter is about taking a step back and looking at the bigger picture. I know you picked up this book because you're somewhere along the path of mastery, career advancement, and exponential income growth. I hope I've shown you ways to achieve that so far.

But there is so much more to life than financial success. True fulfilment comes from creating balance in all areas of your life, from your personal relationships and health to your emotional well-being and sense of purpose.

THE WHEEL OF LIFE: A FRAMEWORK FOR WHOLE-LIFE FULFILMENT

One of the most powerful tools for achieving balance and fulfilment is the **Wheel of Life**. This concept, often used in coaching and personal development, visually represents the different areas that make up a well-rounded life. he Wheel of Life typically includes sections such as:

1. Career/Business
2. Finances
3. Health
4. Family
5. Personal Growth
6. Relationships
7. Fun and Recreation
8. Contribution/Spirituality

Each section represents an important aspect of your life, and the idea is that to live a fulfilling life, you need to focus on all of these areas—not just one or two. Imagine the wheel as a literal wheel—if one section is significantly underdeveloped, the wheel won't turn smoothly. You might have exceptional financial success, but if your health or relationships are neglected, you'll find yourself out of balance.

The Wheel of Life aims to assess your current standing in each area and set goals to improve balance across the board. The more evenly developed each section of your wheel, the smoother and more fulfilling your life journey will be.

MDRT'S WHOLE PERSON CONCEPT: SUCCESS BEYOND FINANCES

Organisations like MDRT understand that financial success is only one part of the equation. That's why MDRT promotes the **Whole Person** concept, which encourages financial advisors to pursue excellence in their professional lives and all areas of life. The Whole Person concept aligns with the Wheel of Life, emphasising the importance of balance in seven key areas: family, health, career, service, education, finances, and personal well-being.

By focusing on these areas, MDRT encourages members to achieve both professional success and personal fulfilment. The idea is that being a "whole person" leads to better outcomes for your career and overall quality of life. It recognises that your family, health, personal growth, and contribution to society are just as important as the commissions you earn or the clients you serve.

THE IMPORTANCE OF WHOLE-LIFE GOALS

Research supports the idea that pursuing goals in multiple areas of life leads to greater fulfilment and long-term happiness. In fact, a study published in the *Journal of Positive Psychology* found that people who set and pursue goals in a variety of life domains—such as career, health, and relationships—experience higher levels of life satisfaction and well-being compared to those who focus solely on professional or financial goals.[14]

This doesn't mean you have to achieve perfection in every area of life all at once. It does mean that if you neglect key aspects of your life for too long, the imbalance will catch up with you. Whether it's a health scare that forces you to slow down or a relationship that suffers due to lack of attention, neglecting other parts of your life can undermine the success you've worked so hard to achieve.

The key to long-term success and fulfilment is to set whole-life goals. These goals encompass every area of your life, ensuring that you're growing in your career and thriving in your relationships, as well as in personal growth and overall well-being. By taking a holistic approach to success, you'll find that each area of your life supports the others, resulting in a more balanced and fulfilling existence.

MY PERSONAL JOURNEY TOWARD WHOLE-LIFE FULFILMENT

This concept hit home during a turning point in my career. In the early years of building my business, I was laser-focused on financial success. I worked long hours, took on every client I could, and pushed myself relentlessly to reach my goals. I said 'yes' to every opportunity without reflecting on which ones were right for me. While I was hitting financial milestones, other areas of my life were being neglected. My health was suffering from the stress, and my time with my family was limited.

It wasn't until I started focusing on my whole life, not just my business, that I found true fulfilment. I realised that success wasn't just about how much money I was making or how many clients I was serving. It was about creating a life that allowed me to enjoy the fruits of my labour. I began setting goals for my health, making time for my family, and pursuing personal growth outside of my business. As my life became more balanced, I found greater success in all areas, including my business.

Today, I continue to set whole-life goals because I understand that true success is about more than just financial achievement. It's about living the life I want to live, being there for the people I love, and taking care of myself in the process.

WHOLE-LIFE GOALS SYSTEM^{IP}: ACTIONABLE STEPS TO SETTING BALANCED GOALS

To help you create a balanced and fulfilling life, I encourage you to set whole-life goals using the Wheel of Life as your guide. Here's how you can do it.

1. ASSESS EACH AREA OF YOUR LIFE

Start by assessing where you currently stand in each area of the Wheel of Life. On a scale of 1 to 10, rate your satisfaction in the following areas:

- Career/Business: _____
- Finances, Health: _____
- Family: _____
- Personal Growth: _____
- Relationships: _____
- Fun and Recreation: _____
- Contribution/Spirituality: _____

This will give you a clear picture of where you're thriving and where you might need to make improvements.

2. SET THREE-MONTH, SIX-MONTH, AND YEARLY GOALS

For each area of your life, set specific goals for the next three months, six months, and for the year. These goals should be SMART—specific, measurable, achievable, relevant, and time-bound. For example:

- **Career/Business:** "Sign three new Right-Fit Clients by March 31" or perhaps even "Say 'NO' to three Wrong-Fit Clients by June 30."
- **Finances:** "Increase savings by 20% by December 31."
- **Health:** "Exercise four times a week and improve my diet by March 31."
- **Family:** "Take a family vacation by June 30."
- **Personal Growth:** "Read 12 personal development books by December 31."
- **Relationships:** "Spend more quality time with my partner by planning regular date nights, such as every Wednesday."
- **Fun and Recreation:** "Start a new hobby and dedicate time to it twice a month."

- **Contribution/Spirituality:** "Volunteer at a local charity once a month until December 31."

3. REVIEW AND ADJUST REGULARLY

Set aside time every few months to review your progress. Are you moving toward your goals in each area of the Wheel of Life? If not, what adjustments can you make? Life is dynamic, and your goals will inevitably evolve over time, so it's essential to remain flexible and make adjustments as needed.

4. CELEBRATE YOUR WINS

Don't forget to celebrate your progress, no matter how small. Whether it's a professional milestone, a personal breakthrough, or a health achievement, recognising your wins will keep you motivated and remind you that you're on the right path.

THE RIPPLE EFFECT OF WHOLE-LIFE SUCCESS

What's powerful about setting whole-life goals is that success in one area often creates a ripple effect that benefits other areas of your life. When you take care of your health, for example, you have more energy and focus to bring to your career. When your relationships are thriving, you feel more supported and motivated to pursue your professional goals.

This is the beauty of pursuing balance—it creates synergy between different parts of your life, leading to greater fulfilment and long-term success. By focusing on the whole picture, you'll achieve more in your career and experience the joy and satisfaction that comes from living a truly well-rounded life.

THE TL;DR VERSION

At the end of the day, financial success is just one piece of the puzzle. It's important, but it's not everything. The real goal is to live a life that you love—a life where you can enjoy the success you've worked so hard to achieve, while also nurturing your relationships, taking care of your health, and growing as a person.

The MDRT's Whole Person concept and the Wheel of Life remind us that success is about more than just the numbers. It's about creating balance, setting whole-life goals, and making sure that as you grow your business, you're also growing in every other area of your life.

So, as you continue your journey toward financial success, don't forget to take care of the things that matter most. Set goals for your whole life, pursue balance and strive for fulfilment in all areas—not just your career. In doing so, you'll create a life that's not only successful but deeply rewarding.

9

TAKE CONTROL–
THE POWER TO SHAPE YOUR LIFE

Imagine waking up every morning with a clear sense of purpose, knowing exactly where you're headed and what steps you need to take to get there. Picture the satisfaction of seeing your hard work, vision, and discipline pay off—not just in your bank account, but in your relationships, health, and personal fulfilment. This is what it means to take control.

But control doesn't come from luck or chance. It's something you claim. It's something you create. And it's available to you right now if you're ready to reach out and take it.

Our world constantly pushes us to focus on the external—on circumstances we can't control, what others think, or fleeting trends. But the truth is, the only control that really matters is internal. The decisions you make, the standards you set, and the actions you take will determine your future. You are the architect of your life. By taking full control, you can build something truly extraordinary.

This isn't about perfection. It's not about having every answer or never making mistakes. Taking control is about something far more empowering; it's about owning your decisions, embracing your potential, and relentlessly pursuing the life you truly want. It's about living with intention and clarity, even when the path ahead feels uncertain.

When you take control, you stop being a passenger in your own life. You take the wheel, set the course, and navigate with purpose. Yes, there will be obstacles. Yes, there will be setbacks. But when you're in control, those challenges don't derail you—they fuel you. They become part of your story, a story of growth, resilience, and triumph.

What does it mean to take control? It means daring to dream bigger than you ever have before. It means refusing to settle for mediocrity or half-measures. It means aligning your actions with your deepest values, your highest aspirations, and the legacy you want to leave behind. The rewards of taking control go far beyond financial success—they touch every area of your life. Your relationships deepen, your health improves, and your self-confidence soars. And most importantly, you experience a profound sense of fulfilment, knowing that you are living life on your terms.

This is your time. The world is full of opportunities, and the only thing standing between you and the life you want is the decision to take control. It doesn't matter where you are today or the challenges you're facing. What matters is where you're willing to go.

SO, WHERE SHOULD YOU BEGIN?

Every journey starts with a single step, and this one is no different. You might feel overwhelmed by everything we've covered right now. There's a lot to think about—your goals, clients, finances, business strategies and tactics, and all of that, in addition to juggling everything else we call 'life.' But don't worry. The path to taking control doesn't require you to master everything overnight. Here's where to start:

1. GET CLEAR ON YOUR GOALS

The first step is always clarity. Without a clear destination, you can't chart a course. So, ask yourself: What do you really want? What are the goals that truly matter to you—not just professionally, but personally as well? Think about the things that excite you, that challenge you, and that push you to grow. Be specific. Write these goals down, and don't hold back. Dream big, but make sure those dreams have deadlines attached to them.

Remember, clear goals aren't just nice ideas; they're essential. They're commitments you make to yourself. They're the promises you keep, even when things get tough. Take the time to visualise the life you want, hitting an income goal, achieving MDRT status, or finding balance in your personal life. This is your roadmap.

2. TAKE OWNERSHIP OF WHERE YOU ARE NOW

Before you can move forward, you need to take stock of where you are today. This isn't about beating yourself up over mistakes or regrets. It's about honestly assessing your current situation. Are you happy with your financial progress? Do you feel fulfilled in your relationships? How's your health? Ownership means recognising that no matter what your circumstances are, you have the power to change them. Own your choices, actions, and responsibility for making the changes you want to see.

3. TAKE A SNAPSHOT: YOUR NUMBERS RIGHT NOW

Once you've set your goals and taken ownership of your current situation, it's time to get specific about the metrics that matter. Your financial, time-based, or personal numbers are the objective feedback that will guide you on this journey.

What do you need to measure to ensure you're moving in the right direction? Set up a system to track your progress. Whether it's your income, client acquisition rates, health goals, or time management, let your numbers tell the truth about how well your strategies are working. Hint: This does NOT need to be elaborate. A simple Excel sheet will do the trick!

4. IDENTIFY YOUR RIGHT-FIT CLIENTS (AND PRIORITIES)

Knowing who you serve is critical, but so is knowing what truly deserves your time and energy. As you build your business, focus on serving the people and nurturing the relationships that align with your values and goals. In the same way, evaluate what aspects of your life—whether it's your health, family, or personal development—deserve priority.

Sometimes, taking control means saying no to the wrong opportunities and people so you can say yes to the right ones. This applies to both your business and personal life.

5. TEST YOUR TACTICS AND REFINE YOUR STRATEGY

No one gets everything right on the first try. Taking control is not about being perfect—it's about being persistent. So, start testing tactics. Try different approaches in your business and your life. Measure what works and what doesn't. And don't be afraid to pivot when necessary. The path to success isn't a straight line—it's filled with adjustments, learning moments, and strategic tweaks. Keep refining your tactics and strategy until you find what works for you.

6. BECOME OBSESSED WITH YOUR GOALS

If you're not completely committed to your goals, you'll find it hard to take control when challenges arise. But obsession doesn't mean unhealthy imbalance—it means engaging wholeheartedly with the process of achieving your goals. It means waking up every day with purpose, pushing through obstacles, and refusing to let distractions steer you off course. Obsession is what fuels long-term success.

7. DON'T LOSE SIGHT OF WHAT MATTERS MOST

Finally, remember that success isn't just about financial achievement. It's about living a life you love. Your health, relationships, and personal well-being are just as important as the numbers in your bank account. As you take control of your career, ensure you're also taking control of your life.

Set whole-life goals that include your family, health, personal growth, and contribution to the world.

Taking control is not a one-time event—it's an ongoing process. It's about being fully present in your own life, making intentional choices, and constantly evolving. Every step you take brings you closer to the life you want, but it all starts with the decision to take control right now.

FINAL WORDS

You've read through the chapters and absorbed the lessons; now it's time to apply them. This journey will be uniquely yours, filled with triumphs, challenges, learning moments, and growth. There will be days when it feels easy, and others when it feels impossible. But through it all, remember that you are in control.

The life you want to live is within reach, and the framework for achieving it is now in your hands. Whether it's scaling your business, achieving your financial goals, or living a life filled with purpose and joy—everything you need is already within you. You have the tools, the knowledge, and the drive. Now, all that's left is the action.

So go out there. Take control of your life, your business, and your future. The world is full of possibilities waiting for you to claim them.

This is your time. The power to create the life you want is in your hands. All you have to do is take control.

RECOMMENDED RESOURCES

PROGRAMS, MEETINGS, AND COURSES

1. Strategic Coach
2. Entrepreneurial Operating System® – For Financial Advisors who see themselves as a business
3. A solid public speaking and communications program
4. MDRT – All the way to MDRT's Top of the Table
5. Coaching programs from

   - Bhupinder Anand – "The Trusted Advisor"
   - Alessandro Forte – "Life, Love & Legacy"

BOOKS, LISTED BY CATEGORY

MINDSET AND IDENTITY

1. *Grit* – Angela Duckworth
2. *Can't Hurt Me* – David Goggins
3. *Be Obsessed or Be Average* – Grant Cardone
4. *Winning* – Tim Grover
5. *Relentless* – Tim Grover
6. *Personality Isn't Permanent* – Benjamin Hardy
7. *The Obstacle Is the Way* – Ryan Holiday

8. *Drive* – Daniel Pink

9. *Start with Why* – Simon Sinek

SYSTEMS, FOCUS, AND EXECUTION

- *Who Not How*® – Dan Sullivan & Dr Benjamin Hardy
- *The 12 Week Year* – Brian Moran
- *Come Up for Air* – Nick Sonnenberg
- Gino Wickman's Books –

  - *Traction*
  - *Rocket Fuel*
  - *Get a Grip*
  - *What the Heck is EOS?*

- *Free to Focus* – Michael Hyatt
- *Deep Work* – Cal Newport (great companion to 12 Week Year)

WEALTH, FINANCIAL STRATEGY, AND BUSINESS THINKING

- *Money: Master the Game* – Tony Robbins
- *The Psychology of Money* – Morgan Housel (great to recommend to clients, too)
- *The Millionaire Fastlane* – MJ DeMarco
- *Rich Dad's CASHFLOW Quadrant* – Robert Kiyosaki (as a business model lens)
- Chad Willardson's Books –

  - *Smart, Not Spoiled*
  - *Beyond the Money*
  - *Fit for Wealth*

ADVISORY EXCELLENCE AND CLIENT RELATIONSHIPS

- *The Trusted Advisor* – David Maister
- *Never Split the Difference* – Chris Voss (for conversations with clients & underwriters alike)
- *Storyworthy* – Matthew Dicks (for becoming a world-class storyteller)
- *Exactly What to Say* – Phil M. Jones (scripts for advisory conversations)
- *Sell with a Story* – Paul Smith (great for speaking and building trust)
- *What Clients Love* – Harry Beckwith (branding + trust in service-based businesses)

PEAK PERFORMANCE

- *Atomic Habits* – James Clear
- *The Gap and the Gain®* – Dan Sullivan & Benjamin Hardy
- *Essentialism* – Greg McKeown
- *Die With Zero* – Bill Perkins (amazing if you're having deeper conversations about life design with HNW clients)

FOR VISIONARY LEADERSHIP AND 10X THINKING

- *Abundance* – Peter Diamandis
- *Bold* – Peter Diamandis
- *The Almanack of Naval Ravikant* – Eric Jorgenson
- *The One Thing* – Gary Keller

FOLLOW RICKSON'S DIGITAL CHANNELS AND CONTENT

| LinkedIn:
Rickson Dsouza | Instagram: @
askrickson | YouTube: @
askrickson | Website:
ricksondsouza.com |

ENDNOTES

1. Edwin A. Locke and Gary P. Latham, *A Theory of Goal Setting and Task Performance* (Englewood Cliffs, NJ: Prentice Hall, 1990).

2. Pierce, Jon L., Tatiana Kostova, and Kurt T. Dirks. "Toward a Theory of Psychological Ownership in Organizations." *The Academy of Management Review* 26, no. 2 (2001): 298–310. https://doi.org/10.2307/259124.

3. Edward L. Deci and Richard M. Ryan. *"Intrinsic Motivation and Self-Determination in Human Behavior."* Plenum Press, 1985.

4. Jocko Willink and Leif Babin, *Extreme Ownership: How U.S. Navy Seals Lead and Win* (New York, NY: St. Martin's Press, 2015).

5. Carol S. Dweck, *Mindset: The New Psychology of Success* (New York, NY: Ballantine Books, 2016).

6. James Clear, *Atomic Habits: An Easy & Proven Way to Build Good Habits & Break Bad Ones* (New York, NY: Avery, 2018).

7. John C. Maxwell, *Failing Forward: Turning Mistakes into Stepping Stones for Success* (HarperCollins Leadership, 2007).

8. Peter F. Drucker. *Management: Tasks, Responsibilities, Practices.* Harper Business, 1993.

9. Neilson, G. L., Martin, K. L., & Powers, E. "The secrets to successful strategy execution." Harvard Business Review, (2008) 86(6), 60–70.

10. Chris McChesney et al., *The 4 Disciplines of Execution: Achieving Your Wildly Important Goals* (New York, NY: Simon & Schuster Paperbacks, an imprint of Simon & Schuster, Inc, 2022).

11. Darren Hardy, *The Compound Effect: Jumpstart Your Income, Your Life, Your Success* (New York, NY: Hachette Go, 2020).

12. Grant Cardone, *Be Obsessed or Be Average* (New York, NY: Portfolio/Penguin, 2016).

13   Cardone, *Be Obsessed.*

14   King, L. A. (2008). "Interventions for enhancing subjective well-being: Can we make people happier and should we?" *The Journal of Positive Psychology*, 3(4), 273–284.

ACKNOWLEDGEMENTS

Thank You

This book is about taking control of your money, your future, your legacy.

But behind every controlled outcome, there's often chaos tamed by community. There are teachers, mentors, challengers, and champions who've shown up in big and small ways.

To those who trusted me to help shape their financial futures, and allowed me to share in their most intimate decisions…

To those who gave me the time, space, and insight to think deeply, write boldly, and speak truthfully…

To those who stood beside me in meeting rooms, on stages, in quiet moments of clarity and chaos…

To Rudolf Dsouza, my father, whose strength through a journey from starting as a bus conductor, from where he started to what he built, has been one of my greatest sources of learning and mentorship.

To Sangeeta, Leiah, and Luca,

To Dan Sullivan and The Strategic Coach Community,

To my Unique Ability® Team,

To my many mentors, like Maurice Serrao and Ashok Sardana,

Thank you.

Your fingerprints are all over these pages.

Lastly, I want to acknowledge those who, often unknowingly, showed up in my life as naysayers. Their skepticism and resistance became unexpected fuel for my drive and determination. For that, I'm equally thankful.

ABOUT THE AUTHOR

Rickson Dsouza is the founder of Successio Global, a Dubai-based succession planning and advisory firm that helps high- and ultra-high-net-worth individuals protect and transition their wealth with clarity and purpose.

With over twenty-five years of experience as of this book's publication, Rickson is a Life Insurance Advisor specialising in legacy and succession planning. He is a 23-year member of the Million Dollar Round Table (MDRT), a 19-year Court of the Table (COT) qualifier, and has achieved Top of the Table (TOT) status for 18 consecutive years since 2009-placing him among the top life insurance advisors globally.

Rickson is also the founder and visionary behind Successio Academy-the home of The Advisors Growth Program (TAGP), a platform designed to equip financial advisors with the tools to build structured, balanced, and purpose-driven practices that fuel exponential professional growth while staying aligned with Whole-Life Goals.

Outside the advisory space, Rickson is a two-time Marathon des Sables (MDS) finisher-a gruelling 250 km ultramarathon across the Sahara Desert, often described as the toughest foot race on Earth-and an Ironman-distance athlete, embodying the endurance and discipline he teaches.

Wherever he goes, Rickson's mission remains constant: to inspire people to live at their full potential. His Unique Ability® lies in futuristic thinking, instigating positive transformation, and driving holistic success-for himself, his clients, and his community.

CONNECT WITH RICKSON

Follow him on your favorite social media platforms today.

RicksonDsouza.com

ARE YOU READY FOR A CHANGE?

KEYNOTE SPEAKER

With years of experience as a business owner, a leading Life Insurance advisor, a Strategic Coach mentee, and having been through a 'whole person' transformation, Rickson encourages others to bring about strategic, holistic change in their lives.

THIS BOOK IS PROTECTED INTELLECTUAL PROPERTY

Instant IP [IP]

The author of this book values Intellectual Property. The book you just read is protected by Instant IP[IP], a proprietary process, which integrates blockchain technology giving Intellectual Property "Global Protection." By creating a "Time-Stamped" smart contract that can never be tampered with or changed, we establish "First Use" that tracks back to the author.

Instant IP [IP] functions much like a Pre-Patent since it provides an immutable "First Use" of the Intellectual Property. This is achieved through our proprietary process of leveraging blockchain technology and smart contracts. As a result, proving "First Use" is simple through a global and verifiable smart contract. By protecting intellectual property with blockchain technology and smart contracts, we establish a "First to File" event.

Protected by Instant IP [IP]

LEARN MORE AT INSTANTIP.TODAY

www.ingramcontent.com/pod-product-compliance
Lightning Source LLC
Chambersburg PA
CBHW071434210326
41597CB00020B/3783